SCIENTIFIC AMERICAN EXPLORES BIG IDEAS

In Concert

HOW MUSIC AFFECTS THE BRAIN

The Editors of *Scientific American*

SCIENTIFIC AMERICAN EDUCATIONAL PUBLISHING

New York

Published in 2024 by Scientific American Educational Publishing
in association with **The Rosen Publishing Group**
2544 Clinton Street, Buffalo NY 14224

Contains material from Scientific American®, a division of Springer Nature America, Inc., reprinted by permission, as well as original material from The Rosen Publishing Group®.

First Edition

Scientific American
Lisa Pallatroni: Project Editor

Rosen Publishing
Erica Grove: Compiling Editor
Michael Moy: Senior Graphic Designer

Cataloging-in-Publication Data

Names: Scientific American, Inc.
Title: In concert: how music affects the brain / edited by the Scientific American Editors.
Description: First Edition. | New York : Scientific American Educational Publishing, 2024. | Series: Scientific American explores big ideas | Includes bibliographic references and index.
Identifiers: ISBN 9781725349667 (pbk.) | ISBN 9781725349674 (library bound)| ISBN 9781725349681 (ebook)
Subjects: LCSH: Music and science–Juvenile literature. | Music–Psychological aspects.
Classification: LCC ML3830.I53 2024 | DDC 781.11–dc23

Manufactured in the United States of America
Websites listed were live at the time of publication.

Cover: Darya Komarova/Shutterstock.com

CPSIA Compliance Information: Batch # SACS24.
For Further Information contact Rosen Publishing at 1-800-237-9932.

CONTENTS

Introduction 6

Section 1: Your Brain on Music 7

1.1 Music Changes the Way You Think 8
By Daniel A. Yudkin and Yaacov Trope

1.2 The Soundtrack of Our Minds 12
By Nikhil Swaminathan

1.3 What Makes a Song? It's the Same Recipe in Every Culture 14
By Jim Daley

1.4 The Beat Goes Off: Scientists Pinpoint the Loss of Musical Perception 18
By Erin Hare

1.5 Music Synchronizes the Brains of Performers and Their Audience 21
By Robert Martone

1.6 Play It Again, Sam 25
By Susana Martinez-Conde

1.7 Exploring the Musical Brain 27
By Kristin Leutwyler

1.8 Music and the Brain 33
By Norman M. Weinberger

1.9 Inner Spark: Using Music to Study Creativity 44
By Alicia Anstead

Section 2: Music and Learning 51

2.1 Music Lessons Combat Poverty's Effect on the Brain 52
By Simon Makin

2.2 Hearing the Music, Honing the Mind 54
By The Editors

2.3 Music Helps Kids Read 56
By Jenni Laidman

2.4 Rhythm and Music Help Math Students 57
By Sophie Bushwick

2.5 Does Music Boost Your Cognitive Performance? 58
By Cindi May

2.6 Everyone Can Gain from Making Music 61
By Julia Calderone

2.7 Fact or Fiction?: Babies Exposed to Classical Music End Up Smarter 65
By Nikhil Swaminathan

2.8 Math, Music, and Imagination 68
By Marcus Miller

2.9 You Don't Have to Start Young to Be a Great Musician 71
By Cindi May

2.10 Even a Few Years of Music Training Benefits the Brain 75
By Christie Wilcox

2.11 Speaking in Tones: Music and Language Partner in the Brain 78
By Diana Deutsch

Section 3: The Healing Power of Music 89

3.1 "Alive Inside" Shows How Music Can Break Through the Fog of Dementia 90
By Annie Sneed

3.2 Heartbeat: Music May Help Keep Your Cardiovascular System in Tune 93
By Lynne Peeples

3.3 Music May Orchestrate Better Brain Connectivity in Preterm Infants 95
By Christopher Intagliata

3.4 How Music Can Literally Heal the Heart 97
By Elaine Chew, Psyche Loui, Grace Leslie, Caroline Palmer, Jonathan Berger, Edward W. Large, Nicolò F. Bernardi, Suzanne Hanser, Julian F. Thayer, Michael A. Casey, and Pier D. Lambiase

3.5 Music Can Heal the Brain 103
By William Forde Thompson and Gottfried Schlaug

Section 4: Play It with Feeling: Music and Emotion 114

4.1 Let's Get Physical: The Psychology of Effective Workout Music 115
By Ferris Jabr

4.2 Why Does Music Make Us Feel? 121
By Mark Changizi

4.3 It's the Bass That Makes Us Boogie 125
By Karen Hopkin

4.4 Is a Sad Song Sad for Everyone? 129
By David Noonan

4.5 Dissecting the Bloodthirsty Bliss of Death Metal 132
By David Noonan

4.6 The Sound of Passion 137
By Patricia Moreau

4.7 Making Creepy Music Gives You Goose Bumps 140
By Amanda Baker

4.8 In Teen Music Choices, Anxiety Rules 143
By Abigail Baird

4.9 Why Music Moves Us 147
By Karen Schrock

Glossary 156

Further Information 157

Citations 158

Index 159

INTRODUCTION

Music has a strong influence over the human brain and the emotional experiences it creates. A soaring score in a movie can evoke strong feelings of fear, sadness, or triumph, depending on the music used. A song can put you to sleep, cause you to remember a past event, or make you feel like dancing. It can create an intense reaction of appreciation or irritation. But what characteristics of music, the human brain, and the way they interact cause these reactions?

Music is a ubiquitous presence across all human cultures, and the discovery of a flute created by our prehistoric ancestors indicates that it goes back to at least 40,000 BCE during the Paleolithic period. The reason for the creation of music is not fully understood, but these facts suggest that it is a fundamental and inherent part of the human experience.

Music has also been established to have a relationship with learning and cognition. Playing a musical instrument has been shown to improve math and problem-solving skills. It stimulates the same parts of the brain as math because it requires critical thinking, learning to read new symbols, and using counting and fractions to keep track of time signatures and rhythm. For similar reasons, it has been demonstrated to improve cognitive skills such as memory in older adults as well. Research indicates that listening to music can also help facilitate healing and improve health by reducing stress and pain.

The articles in this volume will explore these many facets of the relationship between music and the brain. In Section 1, "Your Brain on Music," the articles look at the ways music has been found to influence neurological and psychological activity through considering scientific research. In Section 2, "Music and Learning," authors offer perspectives on the ways music can influence ones mathematical and reading skills, along with cognition and learning more broadly. Section 3, "The Healing Power of Music," looks at research into the health benefits of music. Section 4, "Play It with Feeling: Music and Emotion," takes a deeper dive into the ways music affects emotion.

Section 1: Your Brain on Music

1.1 Music Changes the Way You Think
By Daniel A. Yudkin and Yaacov Trope

1.2 The Soundtrack of Our Minds
By Nikhil Swaminathan

1.3 What Makes a Song? It's the Same Recipe in Every Culture
By Jim Daley

1.4 The Beat Goes Off: Scientists Pinpoint the Loss of Musical Perception
By Erin Hare

1.5 Music Synchronizes the Brains of Performers and Their Audience
By Robert Martone

1.6 Play It Again, Sam
By Susana Martinez-Conde

1.7 Exploring the Musical Brain
By Kristin Leutwyler

1.8 Music and the Brain
By Norman M. Weinberger

1.9 Inner Spark: Using Music to Study Creativity
By Alicia Anstead

Music Changes the Way You Think

By Daniel A. Yudkin and Yaacov Trope

Hum the first two notes of "The Simpsons" theme song. (If you're not a Simpsons fan, "Maria" from *West Side Story* will also do.) The musical interval you're hearing–the pitch gap between the notes–is known as a "tritone," and it's commonly recognized in music theory as one of the most dissonant intervals, so much so that composers and theorists in the 18th century dubbed it *diabolus in musica* ("devil in music").

Now hum the first few notes of "Twinkle Twinkle Little Star," or, if you prefer something with a little more street cred, the "I'm sorry" part in Outkast's "Ms. Jackson." This is the "perfect fifth." It's one of the most consonant intervals, used in myriad compositions as a vehicle of resolution and harmony.

Is it possible that hearing such isolated musical components can change the way you *think*? An ambitious new paper recently published by Jochim Hansen and Johann Melzner in the *Journal of Experimental Social Psychology* argues precisely that. The researchers brought pedestrians into a laboratory and played them a short, stripped-down piece of music consisting of a series of alternating chords. Some people heard chords including the tritone; others the perfect fifth. A couple other tweaks were also made: in the tritone condition, the chords were played slowly–only once every four-beat measure–while in the perfect fifth condition, the chords went by rapidly, sounding every beat. Further, a "reverberation" effect was added such that the tritone chords sounded like they were being played in a cavernous cave and the perfect fifth chords in a carpeted closet.

What the scientists found is that the simple act listening to either of these two chord sets changed how people processed information in a very basic way. For example, the researchers asked people to take a list of shopping items and organize them into groups. Think detergent and paper towels: same kind of thing, or different? Results showed that "tritone" people formed fewer categories than "perfect fifth" people, indicating that they were thinking in broader, more inclusive categories than their counterparts.

In a separate measure, the scientists asked people to imagine buying one of two imaginary toasters. These toasters varied in what is known as "aggregated" versus "individualized" information. Do you know how on Amazon.com you can learn the average star rating of a given item? This is aggregated information; it's pooled from a wide range of sources. Individualized information, by contrast, would be the customer reviews that appear at the bottom of the page. Which do you pay more attention to when these give conflicting messages–when, say, the aggregated information is largely negative but there is a single glowing customer review? Turns out that people who are exposed to "tritone"-type music samples are more likely to be swayed by aggregated information, and "fifth" people by the reverse.

Underlying these seemingly disparate questions is a relatively new theory in social psychology that has shown itself capable of explaining an impressive variety of human behaviors. It's known as construal level theory, and its core premise is that there's a link between how *far* things are from people and how abstractly they construe them. Distant things–a Hawaii vacation next year, say–appear to us general and decontextualized, their basic features (the beach, the sun) forefront in our minds. As they draw near, however, elements we never before considered (the packing, the possibility of rain) suddenly demand our attention. The forest, in other words, becomes the trees. Overall, the theory helps explain many seemingly disparate phenomena, like why we're bad at predicting how long it'll take us to fix the kitchen sink, why absence makes the heart grow fonder, and why we rarely follow through on New Years resolutions. In all these cases, what seemed a certain way from afar turns out, up close, to be a different beast entirely.

How does all this relate to repeating chord patterns? What the researchers have done, cleverly, is consider music's ability to conjure up highly specific mental states. Tiny, almost immeasurable features in a piece of music have the power to elicit deeply personal and specific patterns of thought and emotion in human listeners. (One need only listen to Astrud Gilberto's Grammy-winning performance of the "Girl from Ipanema" to re-appreciate music's ability to capture strange and mysterious moods.) Hansen and Melzner have exploited this fact to provoke in listeners thought patterns corresponding to precisely those mapped by construal level theory.

Ponderous, resonant, unfamiliar tonalities–the proverbial "auditory forest"–cause people to construe things abstractly. By contrast, the rapid, consonant, familiar chords of the perfect fifth–the "auditory trees"–bring out the concrete mindset. The groups of shopping items, the reviews of toasters–these correspond to measures of abstractness that have been developed in experimental psychology. When you group a shopping list into only a few categories, it suggests that you are considering the list abstractly, clustering items according to a common core. And heeding aggregated (versus individualized) information implies the same: you're seeing the forest rather than being swayed by a single tree.

That music can move us is no surprise; it's the point of the art form, after all. What's new here is the manner in which the researchers have quantified in fine-grained detail the cognitive ramifications of unpacked melodic compounds. This investigation of music's building blocks may be more relevant than you suppose. Nowadays, experts in the production room can hone a track–the timbre, tone, rhythm, phrasing–with digital precision. These songwriters and producers are the true geniuses behind the success of popular music today, and they seem to have an intuitive grasp of the phenomena underlying the findings of this psychology article. An extra breath-sound here, a pitch adjustment there–these additives pepper the songs we hear on the radio. So the next time you hear a piece of music from the Billboard Top 40, it may be interesting to wonder, how many components were manipulated *just so*, in order to change the way I think?

About the Authors

Daniel Yudkin is a doctoral candidate in social psychology at New York University and a jazz pianist. He graduated from Williams College, was a Fellow at Harvard University, and once attempted an eleven-country European busking tour funded entirely by street-coins.

Yaacov Trope is a Professor of Psychology at New York University. He received his Ph.D. from the University of Michigan and is a member of the American Association for Arts and Sciences. He has edited several books, including Dual-Process Theories in Social Psychology *(1998),* Self Control in Society, Mind, and Brain *(2010), and* Dual-Process Theories of the Social Mind *(2014). His general areas of interest are social cognition, motivation, and self-control.*

The Soundtrack of Our Minds

By Nikhil Swaminathan

It's a classic cocktail party conundrum: How do our brains decide where we should train our attention when people are milling all about us chatting away–some to us, some to others?

In an attempt to find out, researchers at Stanford University and McGill University in Montreal scanned the brains of 18 subjects who were listening to classical music by 18th-century British composer William Boyce.

"You have to kind of segment these streams [of information] into chunks," says senior study author Vinod Menon, an associate professor of psychiatry and behavioral science at Stanford. The process of slicing the data, he continues, requires that you "identify something that's interesting and then you have to switch on the attentional network."

"Memory doesn't work like video recorder, it's more like DVD," in how it recalls events as discrete chapters, explains study co-author Daniel Levitin, a psychology professor at McGill.

But why music?

Simple, says Sridhar Devarajan, a Stanford neuroscience graduate student involved in the project. "Transitions between musical movements," he notes, "offer an ideal setting to study the dynamically changing landscape of activity in the brain during this segmentation process."

The team wove together different movements from several of Boyce's four- to five-minute symphonies and had volunteers listen to two nine-minute compositions through noise-canceling headphones while lying in an fMRI machine; each of the musical tapestries consisted of 10 orchestral movements. (Boyce's compositions were selected because he is a relatively obscure composer and subjects were less likely to be familiar with his work, canceling out brain activity that would be generated if they had recollections of his symphonies.)

The team conducted full brain scans that allowed them to focus on regions of the brain of particular interest, monitoring them from 10 seconds before a transition between movements to 10 seconds after. (A transition between movements is marked by a decline in the intensity of sound followed by a brief period of silence that leads into a new section of music.)

According to Menon, during the transition periods the team not only observed activity in discrete brain regions, but they also noticed co-active networks (two areas responding simultaneously) reacting to the musical shifts. Activity began in areas in the forward section of the prefrontal cortex of the brain as well as in parts of the temporal cortex just above the brain stem. Menon speculates that it is this network that is "detecting a salient change" in the information stream. Next, areas toward the rear of the prefrontal cortex and parts of the parietal cortex (the outermost layer of the parietal lobe at the upper rear of the brain), began to respond. The regions, Menon notes, are linked to attention and working memory.

"We feel that it could be a very general brain mechanism... part of a core control signal that is generated in response to any attention-demanding task," Menon says. "I think any task that involves detecting a salient event and attending to it will command a similar type of response."

Levitin adds, "Here we had a peak of activation...associated with nothingness," when there was no sound at all. "[Clearly], there are neural processes that are responsible for signaling the beginning and ending of events."

Next up for Menon's team: trying to determine the next level of processing after recognizing and responding to a change in an information stream. It also plans to apply whatever new information it discovers to learn more about "what structure actually means in music."

What Makes a Song? It's the Same Recipe in Every Culture

By Jim Daley

From the first soothing lullabies babies hear to the funereal dirges that accompany the deceased, music is a fixture of the human experience. The latest findings on the cultural basis of singing have ascertained that certain song types—whether lullaby, dance, love, or healing melodies—turn up in all cultures. And each kind of song has common cross-cultural acoustic features.

By analyzing a database of ethnographic descriptions and recordings of songs from around the world, a research team from multiple universities discovered commonalities in acoustic features such as tone, tempo, and pitch. The organization of melodies around a hierarchical chord structure—tonality—appears as a common attribute across all cultures included in the database. Music varies more within than between cultures, indicating that each uses song in the same social context.

The study tries to come to grips with the debate among musicologists as to whether song is a universal human trait that may have deep evolutionary roots. Darwin thought early hominins sang before they developed language, and certain aspects of music appreciation appear to be hardwired in the human brain. "Music is a biological human function, like language is," says Isabelle Peretz, a psychologist at the University of Montreal who was not involved in the study. "As a consequence, music is a universal trait and should exhibit universal properties."

The new research, published Thursday in Science, suggests that humans indeed share a "musical grammar," says psychologist Samuel Mehr, director of the Harvard Music Lab and the study's lead author. "Music is built from similar, simple building blocks the world over," he says.

Mehr and his colleagues compiled 4,709 written accounts of vocal music made by ethnographers and anthropologists over more than a century of research in 60 societies, and combined them with a discography of lullabies, love songs, healing songs, and dances to create a cross-cultural database they dubbed the Natural History of Song (NHS), which is available online. They focused on song because unlike instrumental music, singing is independent of technology and has clear biological underpinnings. They chose four kinds of songs to analyze: lullabies, healing songs, love songs, and dances.

"Our goal was to representatively sample the music that people produce around the world," says study co-author Manvir Singh, an anthropologist at Harvard. "The first thing we had to confront was: How do you represent this music? Ethnomusicologists have rightly critiqued projects that use a single scheme, like representing the world's music in a Western staff because obviously [that] brings all kinds of biases." To avoid this, Singh says, the team used a suite of analytical approaches. They transcribed the songs with Western notation, cataloged them with music information retrieval software and had 30 expert musicologists and hundreds of laypersons listen to and make annotations for excitement and pleasantness and other qualities. They then applied machine classifiers to test whether the identifiable acoustic features of each kind of song predict a song is a lullaby or some other in each of the 60 cultures surveyed.

The analyses revealed that music appears in every culture the researchers observed, and that songs vary primarily in three ways—their formality, religiosity, and arousal (or level of excitement). Those common acoustic features predict the context in which a song is used in every culture they studied. Music also varies along the two dimensions of melodic and rhythmic complexity.

"Humans everywhere share some cognitive mechanism that may have evolved specifically for music, or they may have evolved for mundane purposes like analyzing an auditory environment," Singh says. "On the basis of these cognitive mechanisms, certain songs sound appropriate in certain behavioral contexts."

The researchers took pains to correct for potential biases that any Western ethnographers may have unwittingly brought to their study of non-Western cultures, and noted other possible constraints on their work: experts could have brought their own preconceptions to the annotation process, and the data do not reflect how people in the societies included in the study perceive tonality in their music.

Some musicologists criticized certain aspects of the methodology. "Using Western notation to notate examples and then drawing conclusions from those notated scores is a really problematic practice," says Shannon Dudley, an ethnomusicologist at the University of Washington who was not involved in the study. "Subtleties of rhythm, subtleties of pitch differentiation, articulation and timbre–there are a lot of things that have a huge impact on the way people hear music that aren't there in [Western] notation." Ève Poudrier, a music theorist at the University of British Columbia who was not involved in the study, agrees. Poudrier notes that one of the musical features the researchers mapped to behavioral contexts was whether the song was in a major or minor key. "Major [and] minor is one system of classification of scales that actually is accurate only in Western music," she says.

Mehr says that staff notation was just one of the five methods the researchers used to analyze the songs. "We find the same result each of the five ways–that form and function are linked worldwide," he says. "This suggests that while indeed the transcriptions are missing out on some information related to the singing (like timbre, words, accompanying instruments, etc.), they are nonetheless capturing meaningful information about the vocalizations in the songs." He also says the use of major or minor keys is "simply about the pattern of pitches that are audibly present in the recording. Either they're present or they're not, and it's up to the data to show us whether these features are meaningful in terms of the relation between form and function." Singh adds that no methodology is perfect, and that the NHS data is all open-access. "We'd be glad for anyone to test our conclusions using an alternative method," he says.

W. Tecumseh Fitch, a cognitive biologist at the University of Vienna who was not involved in the study, co-authored an accompanying commentary in *Science*. He says the discovery that musical traits are widespread in humans is consistent with the idea that musicality is very old. "While this [study] certainly doesn't confirm Darwin's proto-language hypothesis, I think it's consistent with the idea that music is very ancient indeed in our species," he says. "It's amazing how diverse it is, but at the same time ... these commonalities are still there."

About the Author

Jim Daley is a freelance journalist from Chicago. He writes about science and health.

The Beat Goes Off: Scientists Pinpoint the Loss of Musical Perception

By Erin Hare

As many as two thirds of stroke victims find themselves suddenly unable to comprehend music. Beyond bad karaoke, these people fundamentally cannot differentiate pitches or rhythms. The medical term is acquired amusia, and recently scientists have aggregated data from of a large group of people with this condition to pinpoint the critical brain regions involved.

A study published in August in *The Journal of Neuroscience* found that the brain is incredibly modular when it comes to the perception of music and speech. Whereas lesions giving rise to deficits in language perception–a condition called aphasia–reside in the brain's left hemisphere, damage associated with amusia are restricted to the right. Aleksi Sihvonen, a neurologist at the University of Turku in Finland and lead author of the study, says he was shocked to see such a clean split. "I think the lateralization was very surprising because the amusic pattern was so clearly in the right," Sihvonen says. "Based on [functional neuroimaging] and left-hemisphere lesion patients who were amusic, we thought there must be [critical music perception circuitry] in the left, too."

According to Steven Sparr, a clinical neurologist at Albert Einstein College of Medicine who was not involved in this study, trying to determine the location of music in the brain has been a long process. It goes back to 1861 when French physician Paul Broca discovered that speech resides entirely within a small circuit in the brain's left hemisphere. So far, there has been no musical lesion case so clean as Broca's, which has led to more than a century of frustration, Sparr says. Yet there were clues that music and language are dissociable. "A little-known fact is that Broca's original patient who was unable to speak was able to sing La Marseillaise [the French national anthem] fluently," Sparr says. "So from the inception of aphasia research [scientists] began to realize that singing and speaking are wired differently."

Why has the neurological evidence to support this notion proved so elusive? According to Sihvonen, it has to do with the case study approach. Given the idiosyncrasy of brain damage patterns as well as the fact that strokes rarely target tissue related to a single function, it can be difficult to draw strong conclusions from small samples.

What sets the present study apart is that it involved 77 participants, making it by far the most extensive of its kind. To identify the lesion locations that are most closely associated with behavioral deficits across subjects, they used a statistical method called voxel-based lesion symptom mapping (VLSM). This methodology allowed the researchers to identify the local nodes that are critically causal for music perception, in contrast to the global network that lights up when healthy people listen to music in a brain scanner. "During a functional neuroimaging scan, we don't know if the brain activation is due to mere musical processing," Sihvonen says. "There can be multiple cognitive processes on top, such as memory, emotions, or reward. That's why [functional] MRI is difficult to interpret."

To be sure that the lateralization of music perception lesions was not merely an artifact of the VLSM statistics, Sihvonen and his colleagues also followed subjects during their recoveries. Both at the time of stroke and six months later, the researchers measured the extent of the lesions across three groups: those without amusia, those who recovered from amusia, and those who remained amusic.

They found that those who remained amusic ultimately ended up losing more brain tissue in the auditory centers of the right hemisphere compared with recovered amusics or nonamusic stroke patients. These results are clinically important because they implicate ongoing atrophy as an important factor in persistent acquired amusia, Sihvonen says. They also reinforce the main finding that the critical areas for music perception are localized in the right hemisphere.

Although this lateralization is clear for the 77 subjects in the study, Sparr points out that only one of them had formal musical training, and prior research indicates the mental representation of music differs vastly for musicians compared with nonmusicians. "The study is very well done and very interesting, but we shouldn't take it as the be-all, end-all, or push the data to say 'we found the musical system of the brain,'" Sparr says. "They found the most common one, but it's certainly not the whole story."

Looking ahead, Sihvonen says he views large-scale lesion studies as just one piece of the puzzle. Different methods ask fundamentally different questions, and a highly complex issue like music perception requires a multifaceted approach. "It's very intriguing to say that the amusia-associated lesions in the right hemisphere represent specific loci for music processing in the brain," Sihvonen says. However, "it most likely involves complex global processes as well."

Music Synchronizes the Brains of Performers and Their Audience

By Robert Martone

When a concert opens with a refrain from your favorite song, you are swept up in the music, happily tapping to the beat and swaying with the melody. All around you, people revel in the same familiar music. You can see that many of them are singing, the lights flashing to the rhythm, while other fans are clapping in time. Some wave their arms over their head, and others dance in place. The performers and audience seem to be moving as one, as synchronized to one another as the light show is to the beat.

A new paper in the journal *NeuroImage* has shown that this synchrony can be seen in the brain activities of the audience and performer. And the greater the degree of synchrony, the study found, the more the audience enjoys the performance. This result offers insight into the nature of musical exchanges and demonstrates that the musical experience runs deep: we dance and feel the same emotions together, and our neurons fire together as well.

In the study, a violinist performed brief excerpts from a dozen different compositions, which were videotaped and later played back to a listener. Researchers tracked changes in local brain activity by measuring levels of oxygenated blood. (More oxygen suggests greater activity, because the body works to keep active neurons supplied with it.) Musical performances caused increases in oxygenated blood flow to areas of the brain related to understanding patterns, interpersonal intentions, and expression.

Data for the musician, collected during a performance, was compared to those for the listener during playback. In all, there were 12 selections of familiar musical works, including "Edelweiss," Franz Schubert's "Ave Maria," "Auld Lang Syne" and Ludwig van Beethoven's "Ode to Joy." The brain activities of 16 listeners were compared to that of a single violinist.

All the musical pieces resulted in synchronization of brain activity between the musician and listener, but this was especially true of the more popular performances. Interbrain coherence was insignificant during the early part of each piece and greatest toward its end. The authors explained that the listener required time to initially understand the musical pattern and was later able to enjoy the performance because it matched that person's expectations.

Synchronous brain activity was localized in the left hemisphere of the brain, to an area known as the temporal-parietal junction. This area is important for empathy, the understanding of others' thoughts and intentions, and verbal working memory used for expressing thought. It may function in the retrieval of sounds and patterns that give rise to musical expectations.

But it is the right brain hemisphere that is most often associated with interpretation of musical melody–in contrast to the left hemisphere, which is specialized for the interpretation of speech. In the right hemisphere, synchronization was localized to areas involved in recognizing musical structure and pattern (the inferior frontal cortex) and interpersonal understanding (the inferior frontal and postcentral cortices). These sites also involve "mirror neurons," brain cells that are thought to enables a mirroring or internalization of others' thoughts and actions.

Mirror neurons both control movement and respond to the sight of it, giving rise to the notion that their activity during passive observation is a silent rehearsal for when they become engaged in active movement. They were once thought to be a biological substrate for mimicry and, more importantly, empathy–the source of our understanding of the actions and intentions of others. Mirror neurons have been faddishly implicated in everything from autism to substance abuse. Nevertheless, nerves that control movement are generally involved in perception as well. And this arrangement is especially true of music, in which physical movement emphasizes melodic gesture or follows a rhythmic beat. Indeed, the auditory cortex enlists other regions of the brain that control movement, showing an innate connection between movement and our understanding of music. No wonder you and your fellow concertgoers dance and move to the music. It is your way of comprehending the music and participating in the encounter.

Because music is a group endeavor, it is often used as the context to study coordinated brain function. Synchronized brain responses among music listeners have been measured by functional magnetic resonance imaging (fMRI) in some studies, while other researchers have examined the coordinated actions of performers by tracking the electrical activities of their brain using electroencephalography. Rather than examine the relationship among groups of performers or groups of listeners, the new *NeuroImage* study examined the relationship between an audience and a performer. And it not only followed the degree of concordance in brain activity among these individuals during a musical encounter but also examined how that concordance was related to musical enjoyment. The brain activity of that person playing air guitar at your concert is closer to that of a true performer than you might have realized.

The various methods used in exploring these relationships have their advantages and shortcomings. For example, the new paper used a technique called functional near-infrared spectroscopy (fNIRS)—which measures the flow of oxygen-rich blood—and it cannot penetrate the brain to investigate deeper structures as well as fMRI does. The major advantage of fNIRS is that no large, expensive instrument is needed so subjects are comparatively unconstrained when they are tested: it would have been impossible for a violinist to play in an MRI machine.

It is remarkable that the observed degree of synchronization between the performer and audience was connected to enjoyment of the music. Such pleasure could provide a powerful means by which music promotes positive social behavior. The pleasantness of music has been attributed to synchronization of electrical activity in the right hemisphere of the brain. Music commands greater attention when it is pleasant, which could contribute to one's feeling of being swept away when listening to a favorite piece. While the authors of the *NeuroImage* paper suggest that the audience's enjoyment was linked to the music matching pattern expectations, other studies have shown that surprise is associated with the greatest degree of musical pleasure. Remarkably, even sad music can bring great enjoyment. For example, Mimì's illness and death in the opera *La Bohème* is filled with tragic sadness, endless regrets, and lost opportunities for redemption, but the music ultimately leads the audience to a bittersweet sense of transcendence.

Whether encountered as a sole listener of a recorded artist or as part of a packed audience before a full orchestra, music is a shared experience that integrates our intellect, emotions, and physical movements. We tap to the beat together and sway in unison to a melody. The experience challenges our cognition to recognize patterns and excites us with pleasure when it surprises us. And we can even enjoy its expression of sadness. Music unites these processes within us and among and between audiences and performers.

About the Author

Robert Martone is a research scientist with expertise in neurodegeneration. He spends his free time kayaking and translating Renaissance Italian literature.

Play It Again, Sam

By Susana Martinez-Conde

In the late 1920s, the friends of the French composer and pianist Maurice Ravel (1875-1937) were becoming concerned about the musician's mental health. Ravel was growing increasingly absent-minded, and his musical scores and letters had started to display uncharacteristic spelling errors. It was during this time period, when Ravel was 53 years old, that he composed his most famous work: *Boléro*.

With only two main themes, each repeated eight times over 340 bars, *Boléro* not only became an audience favorite in Ravel's time, but has sustained great contemporary endurance. Yet, Ravel was not entirely pleased with his creation, and struggled to understand Boléro's success.

Present-day neurologists have speculated that both Ravel's forgetfulness, and the overriding repetition in *Boléro*, were manifestations of frontotemporal dementia, a neurodegenerative disease that may have ultimately caused the composer's death at the age of 62. If so, the early stages of Ravel's dementia might have added to his musical genius, rather than detracted from it.

Ravel might have disagreed. "I've written only one masterpiece – *Boléro*," he once said to the Swiss composer Arthur Honneger. "Unfortunately, there's no music in it."

Is the repetition in *Boléro* extraneous to musicality, as Ravel himself seemed to believe, or an intrinsic part of it? The answer may lie in a new paper, published last week in *Psychonomic Bulletin and Review* by a team of research psychologists at New York University.

Jess Rowland, Anna Kasdan, and David Poeppel conducted a series of experiments to explore whether and how repetition of nonmusical sounds leads to the perception of music. The research built on a previously reported perceptual phenomenon known as the "speech-to-song illusion," in which the repetition of looped speech fragments results in perceived singing.

Rowland and her colleagues wondered whether the speech-to-song illusion might be a particular example of a wide-ranging phenomenon in which auditory repetition–not just of speech sounds, but of sounds overall–leads to the perception of musical structure. To find out, the team presented volunteers with a variety of repetitive audio clips (in which the repeated fragments ranged from 700 milliseconds to 4 seconds), including both speech and the sound of dripping water. The results showed that the musical illusion occurred for both speech and nonspeech sounds, and that it was stronger for the shorter audio fragments.

Two follow-up studies, conducted with musically trained participants, moreover revealed that repetition affected pitch as well as rhythm, indicating a broad phenomenon that may encompass all sorts of auditory materials. The researchers concluded that the formerly described "speech to song" illusion is a specific instantiation of a more general "repetition-to-music" effect.

Ravel famously considered Boléro's entwining repetitions as "orchestral tissue without music." But to our brains, it may be the opposite–repetition might be woven into the very fabric of our melodic experience. If so, it could help explain the *Boléro* earworm that has been coiling my head since I started writing this post.

The views expressed are those of the author(s) and are not necessarily those of Scientific American.

About the Author

Susana Martinez-Conde is a professor of ophthalmology, neurology, and physiology and pharmacology at SUNY Downstate Health Sciences University in Brooklyn, N.Y. She is author of the Prisma Prize–winning Sleights of Mind, *along with Stephen Macknik and Sandra Blakeslee, and of* Champions of Illusion, *along with Stephen Macknik.*

Exploring the Musical Brain

By Kristin Leutwyler

It can bring us to tears or to our feet, drive us into battle or lull us to sleep. Music is indeed remarkable in its power over all humankind. Perhaps for that very reason, no human culture on earth has ever lived without it: people making music predates agriculture and perhaps even language. Take, for instance, the recent discoveries in France and Slovenia of surprisingly sophisticated, sweet-sounding flutes, made by our Neandertal cousins. Some of these instruments, carved from animal bones, are as much as 53,000 years old–more than twice as old as the famed cave paintings in Lascaux.

Despite the ancient and primal nature of music, though, scientists have struggled with some very fundamental questions about its origins and purpose. How does the brain process music? Are there special neural circuits dedicated to creating or interpreting it? If so, are they, like language, unique to human beings? Or do other animals possess true musical ability? Why is an appreciation for music practically universal? Has it conveyed some evolutionary advantage through time? The field of biomusicology is still fairly young, but during the past few years, it has started to answer some of these questions.

Perhaps most basic, researchers have discovered that music like language stimulates many areas in the brain, including regions normally involved in other kinds of thinking. For this reason, Mark Jude Tramo of the Harvard Medical School argues in a recent issue of *Science* that the brain doesn't have a specific "music center," as others have suggested. As an example, he points to the left planum temporale. This tiny brain region is critical to the golden musical gift of perfect pitch: the rare ability to recognize by ear a perfect middle C hit on the piano, or the E of a passing car horn. But the left planum temporale also plays an important role in language processing. Thus, Tramo writes, there is "no grossly identifiable brain structure that works solely during music cognition. However, distinctive patterns of neural activity within the auditory cortex and other areas of the brain may imbue specificity to the processing of music."

Some of the patterns Tramo talks about have revealed themselves through neuroimaging studies–others through tests on patients that, like the subjects of Oliver Sacks's popular books, have suffered unusual forms of brain damage. In the late 1990s, for instance, Isabelle Peretz at the University of Montreal and Catherine Ligeois-Chauvel of INSERM in Marseilles ran several experiments on 65 people who, because of epilepsy, had had part of one or the other temporal lobe surgically removed. From these studies they concluded that musicality resided primarily on one side of the brain: the right hemisphere.

The experiments were simple: Peretz and Ligeois-Chauvel played different songs for each patient twice. Sometimes the melodies were exactly the same. Other times, they had changed in one of several attributes, which researchers describe as "dimensions": first among them is pitch, which pertains to the actual frequency of a particular tone; the second is rhythm, or the duration of series of notes; the third is tempo, the overall pace of a piece; the fourth is contour, which describes the shape of a melody, or its pattern of rises and falls in notes; the fifth is key, or the set of pitches to which notes in a melody belong; other dimensions include timbre, loudness, and spatial location.

The scientists found that people with damage to the left temporal lobe had difficulty recognizing changes only in key, whereas those with damage to the right side struggled to recognize changes in both key and contour. Later imaging studies showed a similar bias toward the right hemisphere–particularly among nonmusicians–although Tramo notes that more recent work calls some of this "musical hemisphere" hypothesis into question. "The belt and parabelt areas [of the auditory cortex] in the right hemisphere discriminate local changes in note duration and separation," he writes, "whereas grouping by meter involves mostly anterior parabelt areas in both hemispheres."

From Mind's Eye to Emotion's Seat

For certain, it is becoming apparent that unexpected and unsophisticated areas of the brain are sometimes involved in interpreting, writing, feelin,g or performing music. As some research has showed, even the visual cortex sometimes gets into the act. Herv Platel, Jean-Claude Baron and their colleagues at the University of Caen used positron emission tomography (PET) to monitor the effects of changes in pitch. What they found much to their surprise was that Brodmann's areas 18 and 19 in the visual cortex lit up. These areas are better known as the "mind's eye" because they are, in essence, our imagination's canvas. Any make-believe picture begins there. Thus, Baron suggests that the brain may create a symbolic image to help it decipher changes in pitch.

But music goes much deeper than that below the outer layers of the auditory and visual cortex to the limbic system, which controls our emotions. The emotions generated there produce a number of well-known physiological responses. Sadness, for instance, automatically causes pulse to slow, blood pressure to rise, a drop in the skin's conductivity, and a rise in temperature. Fear increases heart rate; happiness makes you breathe faster. By monitoring such physical reactions, Carol Krumhansl of Cornell University demonstrated that music directly elicits a range of emotions. Music with a quick tempo in a major key, she found, brought about all the physical changes associated with happiness in listeners. In contrast, a slow tempo and minor key led to sadness.

Robert Zatorre and Anne Blood at McGill University corroborated Krumhansl's findings with PET imaging experiments. They created original melodies containing dissonant and consonant patterns of notes, and played them for a group of volunteers willing to be scanned at the same time. As expected, dissonance made areas of the limbic system linked to unpleasant emotions light up in the PET scans, whereas the consonant melodies stimulated limbic structures associated with pleasure.

That music strikes such a chord with the limbic system—an ancient part of our brain, evolutionarily speaking, and one that we share with much of the animal kingdom—is no accident, some researchers assert. In another recent paper in *Science*, Patricia Gray, head of the biomusic program at the National Academy of the Sciences, and several colleagues from around the country propose that music came into this world long before the human race ever did. "The fact that whale and human music have so much in common even though our evolutionary paths have not intersected for 60 million years," they write, "suggests that music may predate humans—that rather than being the inventors of music, we are latecomers to the musical scene."

Humpbacks, Hummingbirds, and Human Composers

Gray and company note that humpback composers employ many of the same tricks human songwriters do. In addition to using similar rhythms, humpbacks keep musical phrases to a few seconds, creating themes out of several phrases before singing the next one. Whale songs in general are no shorter than human ballads and no longer than symphony movements, perhaps because they have a similar attention span. Even though they can sing over a range of seven octaves, the whales typically sing in key, spreading adjacent notes no farther apart than a scale. They mix percussive and pure tones in pretty much the same ratios as human composers and follow their ABA form, in which a theme is presented, elaborated on, and then revisited in a slightly modified form.

Perhaps most amazing, humpback whale songs include repeating refrains that rhyme. Gray and her colleagues say that whales might use rhymes for exactly the same reasons we do: as devices to help them remember. As a recent study showed, whale songs are often rather catchy. When a few humpbacks from the Indian Ocean strayed into the Pacific, some of the whales they met there quickly changed their tunes singing the new whales' songs within three short years.

Back on land, birds, too, make music much like people. "When birds compose songs they often use the same rhythmic variations, pitch relationships, permutations, and combinations of notes as human composers," Gray and her colleagues write, citing work done by their late co-author Luis Baptista. "Thus, some bird songs resemble musical compositions; for example, the canyon wren's trill cascades down the musical scale lie the opening of Chopin's 'Revolutionary' Etude." That same bird sings in the chromatic scale, which divides the octave into 12 semitones, and the hermit thrush sings in the so-called pentatonic scale. It is perhaps because these birds pitch their songs to the same scale as Western music that people find them so attractive.

Why would such different creatures with such different physical means for making sound all adopt such astonishingly uniform patterns for their melodies? Gray and her colleagues conclude that the similarities "tempt one to speculate that the platonic alternative may exist that there is a universal music awaiting discovery." But in fact, there is currently considerable debate over the purpose of music, and whether it was adaptive for humans in evolution or not.

"Auditory Cheesecake" or Evolutionary Advantage?

Linguist Steven Pinker of the Massachusetts Institute of Technology has proposed that music is merely "auditory cheesecake," or "an evolutionary accident piggy-backing on language," as Daniel J. Levitin at McGill University explained in a recent issue of the journal *Cerebrum*. But many scientists Levitin among them don't agree. "Some researchers are finding that listening to familiar music activates neural structures deep in the ancient primitive regions of the brain, the cerebellar vermis," Levitin writes. "For music so profoundly to affect this gateway to emotion, it must have some ancient and important function."

Geoffrey Miller of University College London has proposed that musical ability–like broad shoulders or showy plumes–may serve to demonstrate fitness to a potential mate. After all, singing or playing an instrument well requires dexterity and good memory. Another suggestion Levitin makes is that music functions as communication, perhaps mimicking the rhythm and contour of our species' primitive calls. So, too, he proposes that perhaps music conveys an advantage through stimulating our primitive timing mechanisms.

Most interesting, he suggests that music stimulates our drive to find patterns in the environment. "Our brain is constantly trying to make order out of disorder, and music is a fantastic pattern game for our higher cognitive centers," he writes. "From our culture, we learn (even if unconsciously) about musical structures, tones, and other ways of understanding music as it unfolds over time; and our brains are exercised by extracting different patterns and groupings from music's performance." It is this very kind of pattern recognition, which is extremely important for making sense of the world around us that Keith Devlin suggests in his book *The Math Gene* gave rise to language and stands behind mathematical ability as well. To be certain, researchers won't agree on the purpose of music anytime soon, which fortunately shouldn't stop any of us from enjoying it.

Music and the Brain

By Norman M. Weinberger

Music surrounds us–and we wouldn't have it any other way. An exhilarating orchestral crescendo can bring tears to our eyes and send shivers down our spines. Background swells add emotive punch to movies and TV shows. Organists at ballgames bring us together, cheering, to our feet. Parents croon soothingly to infants.

And our fondness has deep roots: we have been making music since the dawn of culture. More than 30,000 years ago early humans were already playing bone flutes, percussive instruments, and jaw harps—and all known societies throughout the world have had music. Indeed, our appreciation appears to be innate. Infants as young as two months will turn toward consonant, or pleasant, sounds and away from dissonant ones. And the same kinds of pleasure centers light up in a person's brain whether he or she is getting chills listening to a symphony's denouement or eating chocolate or having sex or taking cocaine.

Therein lies an intriguing biological mystery: Why is music–universally beloved and uniquely powerful in its ability to wring emotions–so pervasive and important to us? Could its emergence have enhanced human survival somehow, such as by aiding courtship, as Geoffrey F. Miller of the University of New Mexico has proposed? Or, as suggested by Robin I. M. Dunbar of the University of Liverpool in England, did it originally help us by promoting social cohesion in groups that had grown too large for grooming? On the other hand, to use the words of Harvard University's Steven Pinker, is music just auditory cheesecake–a happy accident of evolution that happens to tickle the brain's fancy?

Neuroscientists don't yet have the ultimate answers. But in recent years we have begun to gain a firmer understanding of where and how music is processed in the brain, which should lay a foundation for answering evolutionary questions. Collectively, studies of patients with brain injuries and imaging of healthy individuals have unexpectedly uncovered no specialized brain center for music. Rather music engages many areas distributed throughout the brain, including those that are usually involved in other kinds of cognition. The active areas vary with the person's individual experiences and musical training. The ear has the fewest sensory cells of any sensory organ--3,500 inner hair cells occupy the ear versus 100 million photoreceptors in the eye. Yet our mental response to music is remarkably adaptable; even a little study can retune the way the brain handles musical inputs.

Inner Songs

Until the advent of modern imaging techniques, scientists gleaned insights about the brain's inner musical workings mainly by studying patients--including famous composers--who had experienced brain deficits as a result of injury, stroke, or other ailments. For example, in 1933 French composer Maurice Ravel began to exhibit symptoms of what might have been focal cerebral degeneration, a disorder in which discrete areas of brain tissue atrophy. His conceptual abilities remained intact--he could still hear and remember his old compositions and play scales. But he could not write music. Speaking of his proposed opera *Jeanne d'Arc*, Ravel confided to a friend, "... this opera is here, in my head. I hear it, but I will never write it. It's over. I can no longer write my music." Ravel died four years later, following an unsuccessful neurosurgical procedure. The case lent credence to the idea that the brain might not have a specific center for music.

The experience of another composer additionally suggested that music and speech were processed independently. After suffering a stroke in 1953, Vissarion Shebalin, a Russian composer, could no longer talk or understand speech, yet he retained the ability to write music until his death 10 years later. Thus, the supposition of independent processing appears to be true, although more recent work has yielded a more nuanced understanding, relating to two of the features that music and language share: both are a means of communication, and each has a syntax, a set of rules that govern the proper combination of elements (notes and words, respectively). According to Aniruddh D. Patel of the Neurosciences Institute in San Diego, imaging findings suggest that a region in the frontal lobe enables proper construction of the syntax of both music and language, whereas other parts of the brain handle related aspects of language and music processing.

Imaging studies have also given us a fairly fine-grained picture of the brain's responses to music. These results make the most sense when placed in the context of how the ear conveys sounds in general to the brain. Like other sensory systems, the one for hearing is arranged hierarchically, consisting of a string of neural processing stations from the ear to the highest level, the auditory cortex. The processing of sounds, such as musical tones, begins with the inner ear (cochlea), which sorts complex sounds produced by, say, a violin, into their constituent elementary frequencies. The cochlea then transmits this information along separately tuned fibers of the auditory nerve as trains of neural discharges. Eventually these trains reach the auditory cortex in the temporal lobe. Different cells in the auditory system of the brain respond best to certain frequencies; neighboring cells have overlapping tuning curves so that there are no gaps. Indeed, because neighboring cells are tuned to similar frequencies, the auditory cortex forms a frequency map across its surface.

The response to music per se, though, is more complicated. Music consists of a sequence of tones, and perception of it depends on grasping the relations between sounds. Many areas of the brain are involved in processing the various components of music. Consider tone, which encompasses both the frequencies and loudness of a sound. At one time, investigators suspected that cells tuned to a specific frequency always responded the same way when that frequency was detected.

But in the late 1980s David Diamond, Thomas M. McKenna and I, working in my laboratory at the University of California, Irvine, raised doubts about that notion when we studied contour, which is the pattern of rising and falling pitches that is the basis for all melodies. We constructed melodies consisting of different contours using the same five tones and then recorded the responses of single neurons in the auditory cortices of cats. We found that cell responses (the number of discharges) varied with the contour. Responses depended on the location of a given tone within a melody; cells may fire more vigorously when that tone is preceded by other tones rather than when it is the first. Moreover, cells react differently to the same tone when it is part of an ascending contour (low to high tones) than when it is part of a descending or more complex one. These findings show that the pattern of a melody matters: processing in the auditory system is not like the simple relaying of sound in a telephone or stereo system.

Most research has focused on melody, but rhythm (the relative lengths and spacing of notes), harmony (the relation of two or more simultaneous tones), and timbre (the characteristic difference in sound between two instruments playing the same tone) are also of interest. Studies of rhythm have concluded that one hemisphere is more involved, although they disagree on which hemisphere. The problem is that different tasks and even different rhythmic stimuli can demand different processing capacities. For example, the left temporal lobe seems to process briefer stimuli than the right temporal lobe and so would be more involved when the listener is trying to discern rhythm while hearing briefer musical sounds.

The situation is clearer for harmony. Imaging studies of the cerebral cortex find greater activation in the auditory regions of the right temporal lobe when subjects are focusing on aspects of harmony. Timbre also has been assigned a right temporal lobe preference. Patients whose temporal lobe has been removed (such as to eliminate seizures) show deficits in discriminating timbre if tissue from the right, but not the left, hemisphere is excised. In addition, the right temporal lobe becomes active in normal subjects when they discriminate between different timbres.

Brain responses also depend on the experiences and training of the listener. Even a little training can quickly alter the brain's reactions. For instance, until about 10 years ago, scientists believed that tuning was fixed for each cell in the auditory cortex. Our studies on contour, however, made us suspect that cell tuning might be altered during learning so that certain cells become extra sensitive to sounds that attract attention and are stored in memory.

To find out, Jon S. Bakin, Jean-Marc Edeline and I conducted a series of experiments during the 1990s in which we asked whether the basic organization of the auditory cortex changes when a subject learns that a certain tone is somehow important. Our group first presented guinea pigs with many different tones and recorded the responses of various cells in the auditory cortex to determine which tones produced the greatest responses. Next, we taught the subjects that a specific, nonpreferred tone was important by making it a signal for a mild foot shock. The guinea pigs learned this association within a few minutes. We then determined the cells' responses again, immediately after the training and at various times up to two months later. The neurons' tuning preferences had shifted from their original frequencies to that of the signal tone. Thus, learning retunes the brain so that more cells respond best to behaviorally significant sounds. This cellular adjustment process extends across the cortex, editing the frequency map so that a greater area of the cortex processes important tones. One can tell which frequencies are important to an animal simply by determining the frequency organization of its auditory cortex.

The retuning was remarkably durable: it became stronger over time without additional training and lasted for months. These findings initiated a growing body of research indicating that one way the brain stores the learned importance of a stimulus is by devoting more brain cells to the processing of that stimulus. Although it is not possible to record from single neurons in humans during learning, brain-imaging studies can detect changes in the average magnitude of responses of thousands of cells in various parts of the cortex. In 1998 Ray Dolan and his colleagues at University College London trained human subjects in a similar type of task by teaching them that a particular tone was significant. The group found that learning produces the same type of tuning shifts seen in animals. The long-term effects of learning by retuning may help explain why we can quickly recognize a familiar melody in a noisy room and also why people suffering memory loss from neurodegenerative diseases such as Alzheimer's can still recall music that they learned in the past.

Even when incoming sound is absent, we all can listen by recalling a piece of music. Think of any piece you know and play it in your head. Where in the brain is this music playing? In 1999 Andrea R. Halpern of Bucknell University and Robert J. Zatorre of the Montreal Neurological Institute at McGill University conducted a study in which they scanned the brains of nonmusicians who either listened to music or imagined hearing the same piece of music. Many of the same areas in the temporal lobes that were involved in listening to the melodies were also activated when those melodies were merely imagined.

Well-Developed Brains

Studies of musicians have extended many of the findings noted above, dramatically confirming the brain's ability to revise its wiring in support of musical activities. Just as some training increases the number of cells that respond to a sound when it becomes important, prolonged learning produces more marked responses and physical changes in the brain. Musicians, who usually practice many hours a day for years, show such effects—their responses to music differ from those of nonmusicians; they also exhibit hyperdevelopment of certain areas in their brains.

Christo Pantev, then at the University of Mnster in Germany, led one such study in 1998. He found that when musicians listen to a piano playing, about 25 percent more of their left hemisphere auditory regions respond than do so in nonmusicians. This effect is specific to musical tones and does not occur with similar but nonmusical sounds. Moreover, the authors found that this expansion of response area is greater the younger the age at which lessons began. Studies of children suggest that early musical experience may facilitate development. In 2004 Antoine Shahin, Larry E. Roberts, and Laurel J. Trainor of McMaster University in Ontario recorded brain responses to piano, violin and pure tones in four- and five-year-old children. Youngsters who had received greater exposure to music in their homes showed enhanced brain auditory activity, comparable to that of unexposed kids about three years older.

Musicians may display greater responses to sounds, in part because their auditory cortex is more extensive. Peter Schneider and his co-workers at the University of Heidelberg in Germany reported in 2002 that the volume of this cortex in musicians was 130 percent larger. The percentages of volume increase were linked to levels of musical training, suggesting that learning music proportionally increases the number of neurons that process it.

In addition, musicians' brains devote more area toward motor control of the fingers used to play an instrument. In 1995 Thomas Elbert of the University of Konstanz in Germany and his colleagues reported that the brain regions that receive sensory inputs from the second to fifth (index to pinkie) fingers of the left hand were significantly larger in violinists; these are precisely the fingers used to make rapid and complex movements in violin playing. In contrast, they observed no enlargement of the areas of the cortex that handle inputs from the right hand, which controls the bow and requires no special finger movements. Nonmusicians do not exhibit these differences. Further, Pantev, now at the Rotman Research Institute at the University of Toronto, reported in 2001 that the brains of professional trumpet players react in such an intensified manner only to the sound of a trumpet–not, for example, to that of a violin.

Musicians must also develop greater ability to use both hands, particularly for keyboard playing. Thus, one might expect that this increased coordination between the motor regions of the two hemispheres has an anatomical substrate. That seems to be the case. The anterior corpus callosum, which contains the band of fibers that interconnects the two motor areas, is larger in musicians than in nonmusicians. Again, the extent of increase is greater the earlier the music lessons began. Other studies suggest that the actual size of the motor cortex, as well as that of the cerebellum–a region at the back of the brain involved in motor coordination–is greater in musicians.

Ode to Joy—or Sorrow

Beyond examining how the brain processes the auditory aspects of music, investigators are exploring how it evokes strong emotional reactions. Pioneering work in 1991 by John A. Sloboda of Keele University in England revealed that more than 80 percent of sampled adults reported physical responses to music, including thrills, laughter,or tears. In a 1995 study by Jaak Panksepp of Bowling Green State University, 70 percent of several hundred young men and woman polled said that they enjoyed music because it elicits emotions and feelings. Underscoring those surveys was the result of a 1997 study by Carol L. Krumhansl of

Cornell University. She and her coworkers recorded heart rate, blood pressure, respiration, and other physiological measures during the presentation of various pieces that were considered to express happiness, sadness, fear, or tension. Each type of music elicited a different but consistent pattern of physiological change across subjects.

Until recently, scientists knew little about the brain mechanisms involved. One clue, though, comes from a woman known as I.R. (initials are used to maintain privacy) who suffered bilateral damage to her temporal lobes, including auditory cortical regions. Her intelligence and general memory are normal, and she has no language difficulties. Yet she can make no sense of nor recognize any music, whether it is a previously known piece or a new piece that she has heard repeatedly. She cannot distinguish between two melodies no matter how different they are. Nevertheless, she has normal emotional reactions to different types of music; her ability to identify an emotion with a particular musical selection is completely normal! From this case we learn that the temporal lobe is needed to comprehend melody but not to produce an emotional reaction, which is both subcortical and involves aspects of the frontal lobes.

An imaging experiment in 2001 by Anne Blood and Zatorre of McGill sought to better specify the brain regions involved in emotional reactions to music. This study used mild emotional stimuli, those associated with people's reactions to musical consonance versus dissonance. Consonant musical intervals are generally those for which a simple ratio of frequencies exists between two tones. An example is middle C (about 260 hertz, or Hz) and middle G (about 390 Hz). Their ratio is 2:3, forming a pleasant-sounding perfect fifth interval when they are played simultaneously. In contrast, middle C and C sharp (about 277 Hz) have a complex ratio of about 17:18 and are considered unpleasant, having a rough sound.

What are the underlying brain mechanisms of that experience? PET (positron-emission tomography) imaging conducted while subjects listened to consonant or dissonant chords showed that different localized brain regions were involved in the emotional reactions. Consonant chords activated the orbitofrontal area (part of the reward system) of the right hemisphere and also part of an area below the corpus callosum. In contrast, dissonant chords activated the right parahippocampal gyrus. Thus, at least two systems, each dealing with a different type of emotion, are at work when the brain processes emotions related to music. How the different patterns of activity in the auditory system might be specifically linked to these differentially reactive regions of the hemispheres remains to be discovered.

In the same year, Blood and Zatorre added a further clue to how music evokes pleasure. When they scanned the brains of musicians who experienced chills of euphoria when listening to music, they found that music activated some of the same reward systems that are stimulated by food, sex, and addictive drugs.

Overall, findings to date indicate that music has a biological basis and that the brain has a functional organization for music. It seems fairly clear, even at this early stage of inquiry, that many brain regions participate in specific aspects of music processing, whether supporting perception (such as apprehending a melody) or evoking emotional reactions. Musicians appear to have additional specializations, particularly hyperdevelopment of some brain structures. These effects demonstrate that learning retunes the brain, increasing both the responses of individual cells and the number of cells that react strongly to sounds that become important to an individual. As research on music and the brain continues, we can anticipate a greater understanding not only about music and its reasons for existence but also about how multifaceted it really is.

About the Author

Norman M. Weinberger, who received his Ph.D. in experimental psychology from Western Reserve University, works in the department of neurobiology and behavior at the University of California, Irvine. He is a founder of U.C.I.'s

Center for the Neurobiology of Learning and Memory and of MuSICA (Music and Science Information Computer Archive). A pioneer in the field of learning and memory in the auditory system, Weinberger is on the editorial board of the journal Neurobiology of Learning and Memory.

Inner Spark: Using Music to Study Creativity

By Alicia Anstead

Charles J. Limb might have been a jazz saxophonist. He grew up in a musical family and showed early signs of talent. He idolized John Coltrane and, as a student at Harvard, directed a jazz band. Although he ultimately went to medical school, he chose his specialty (otolaryngology) in part because of his musical interest. As a hearing specialist and surgeon at Johns Hopkins Medical Center, he performs cochlear implants in patients to restore hearing and enable the deaf to appreciate music. His sensibility and passion as an artist continue to inform his research. At least half of his studies during the past 10 years have focused on regions of the brain activated during moments of deep creativity. As he puts it, he wants to understand what went on in Coltrane's head when he performed brilliant improv on his sax night after night.

Limb and National Institutes of Health neurologist Allen R. Braun have developed a method for studying the brains of highly skilled jazz musicians while they are creating music. Subjects play on a nonmagnetic keyboard as they lie in a functional magnetic resonance imaging (fMRI) machine that takes pictures of their brain. Then the scientists compare neural activity during improvisation with what happens when playing a memorized piece. Limb can also interact with the musician in the scanner by playing on an external keyboard–or, as musicians put it, exchanging riffs.

Limb's work is fueled in part by a determination to understand the implications for transforming education and for encouraging everyone to live purposely creative lives. Excerpts follow:

Q: Why should scientists study creativity?

A: While I think creativity is amazing, I don't put it on a pedestal. I view at it as a very normal biological process that some people are able to take to extremely profound levels but that fundamentally is a basic requirement of human civilization and how we advance. It infiltrates every aspect of human life. I don't know that there's an attribute that is more responsible for how we've evolved as a species than creativity.

From a scientific perspective: if it's a biological behavior, if humans are creative beings, we really ought to study it like you study any other complex biological behavior. Furthermore, because it does seem to be important, not just for the arts but for life, it's probably something we should understand better.

Q: Why is improvisation an ideal activity for studying creativity?

A: There are a lot of forms of creativity. For scientific study, what you really need is the behavior that is a prototypical creative act, realizing that it doesn't represent all creative behavior. Writing a novel is a creative act, but it's hard to do that in an fMRI scanner, and something that takes a year or so to do is hard to study. Musical improvisation is spontaneous. The timescale is relatively concise, meaning that every time you do it, you can constrain it to a time frame quite reasonably and expect artistically relevant results. That's a natural task for a musician. So the timescale is natural for a scientific experiment.

Q: What kinds of challenges did you face in trying to summon creativity on demand? Musicians don't usually find a muse in a science lab.

A: The musicians were a self-selected bunch. I didn't coerce them to participate. They were all into the idea. The experience is foreign for the first minute or two, and then it becomes surprisingly comfortable. You're in a tube, and it's dark, and you have only headphones–it's almost like a sensory deprivation chamber where the only thing you're doing is playing piano. It's really a strange environment for playing piano, but there's not a lot to distract you. In fact, I think the music is very comforting in that setting because it's the one normal thing about the setting.

The sound quality of the piano we used isn't the best. It's noisy as heck in that room. But none of the musicians complained, and they were able to play pretty well. Sometimes musicians felt embarrassed that they weren't able to play the way they normally play, but from my perspective they played very well.

Q: Tell us about the keyboard you used in your experiments and how you adapted it to work with fMRI.

A: The main issues to do this are ergonomic and magnetic. You have to have a keyboard that works when you're in a narrow tube, on your back. I went into the scanner myself many times and thought about what would be the best way to make this work out. We decided the piano should be on your lap, with your hands at a natural angle in front of you, but your eyes—because you're lying down—could not be looking down. We used mirrors, so you look up at one mirror that points to another mirror that is pointed at the keyboard. In the end, you're looking at your hands even though you're looking straight ahead.

The dimension of the tube is such that we could have only 35 keys. I wanted to make them full-size so that the players would feel relatively natural. I was working with an engineer who designs MRI-compatible devices, and he and I shipped this device across the country probably 10 times to tweak it. It was a two-year process. What we had to design was a MIDI keyboard—for musical instrument digital interface—so the piano makes no noise. Every time you press a note, it sends a digital message to a computer saying a certain note was pressed. I used a program called Logic Pro, which has a piano emulator. When you press a certain note, the computer program plays the note back through headphones. When you're doing it, it feels very much like you're playing a piano naturally.

Q: What happens neurologically to the brain during creativity?

A: As far as my studies have revealed, creativity is a whole-brain activity. When you're doing something that's creative, you're engaging all aspects of your brain. During improvisation, the prefrontal cortex of the brain undergoes an interesting shift in activity, in which a broad area called the lateral prefrontal region shuts down, essentially so you have a significant inhibition of your prefrontal cortex. These areas are involved in conscious self-monitoring, self-inhibition, and evaluation of the rightness and wrongness of actions you're about to implement. In the meantime, we saw another area of the prefrontal cortex–the medial prefrontal cortex–turn on. This is the focal area of the brain that's involved in self-expression and autobiographical narrative. It's part of what is known as a default network. It has to do with sense of self.

Q: What implications does your work have for, say, education?

A: If we can understand what actually changes in the brain to perhaps reduce conscious self-monitoring–what a lot of expert musicians are doing and what amateur musicians are unable to do–that's a pretty interesting target for someone to consider when trying to learn to become an improviser. I think that has implications for describing what gives rise to excellent improvisation and what experts do naturally. How a teacher can take that and utilize it in a lesson is another thing entirely, but I think there's food for thought.

Q: A number of researchers are investigating creativity right now. Why do you think this convergence of interest is taking place?

A: We have some new methods of analyzing brain activity and brain function that are allowing us to ask questions that were probably off-limits for scientists. And I think that says a lot about the way scientists are in general. Scientists are, for the most part, a pretty conservative bunch. They're not the kinds that want to answer the riskiest questions in terms of art. There are too many variables, it's hard to explain, and there's not a lot of grant funding. It's not disease-based, etcetera. Now we are seeing that, okay, these are legitimate questions to ask, and we have legitimate methods to try to answer the questions. We need to learn how creativity affects the brain and how to implement creativity in educational systems, how to encourage children to be creative.

Q: How do you respond to skeptics and critics who call fMRI research high-tech phrenology?

A: That's an interesting criticism. There's a big difference between saying that the scalp is shaped a certain way and saying that an area of the brain is physiologically active. What we're really trying to do is take a glimpse into an artist's brain while he is doing something that is unique. Keep in mind the method we use for this–fMRI–is a very, very inferential method. It is completely imprecise on so many levels, and at best you are inferring a pattern of activity that is associated with a pattern of behavior. Every method has its intrinsic limits, and that's how it should be. And in the end, what you want or hope for is that a lot of different methods, not just fMRI, are applied to the same question so that you can see converging data.

There's a reason why we're using fMRI, however. It shows us a lot of things that we've never been able to actually see before, which is human behavior in its most complex forms happening in real time. But I'm a very big critic of anyone who thinks fMRI holds the answer to everything. Having used it, I know it doesn't. On the other hand, that doesn't mean that we shouldn't extract what we can. I mean, it's a cool method.

Q: What are the implications of your creativity research for your work as a surgeon and for cochlear implants?

A: In truth, the reason why I do what I do is because I love music. That is why I wanted to become a hearing specialist. That led me to treat surgical disorders of hearing primarily. Cochlear implantation is probably the best treatment that has ever existed for a profound sensory impairment, meaning there is no other sense that can be restored right now like hearing can be with a cochlear implant. These things are amazing technologically. Yet they're also very limited. What they are amazing at is producing language for people who have had intact hearing for most of their lives or for people who are born deaf and gain hearing through implants.

But music is another piece entirely. Most people who have a cochlear implant just can't hear music well. A large portion of my research goes toward trying to understand the limitations of music perception in deaf people who are hearing with cochlear implants. And I'm hoping to try to improve that. So that is a large part of what I study as well.

For me, the two parts of my work are motivated by the same idea of bringing the sublime to the deaf. The idea of going from deaf to Beethoven's Symphony no. 9 is pretty remarkable. I would love to be able take somebody there.

Q: What's next in your creativity research?

A: The "trading fours" research, in which I exchange riffs with a musician in the scanner, is still ongoing, as are the studies of freestyle rappers, which I believe represents the first-ever neuroscientific study of hip-hop. The next real direction I'm headed into has to do with trying to clarify our study of reward mechanisms in the brain and their relation to creativity. Why is it that we like to be creative? Why is it that we like to perceive creativity? And what happens when somebody is improvising in terms of pleasure or reward centers? Where is the gratification neurologically, and how does that change according to the emotional content of the music? I've always wondered: Why do we love sad music? Why does it make us feel better and not worse? It's a funny inversion that takes place in the brain. Whereas we try to avoid sadness in life, in art, and especially in music, we almost gravitate toward it. By and large, the effect is very positive. Improvisation causes a similar response: When you're spontaneously creating music that is sad, what are you getting? Are you getting joy? Pleasure? What's the basis of the reward? That's one of the directions I'm heading.

Q: What's your best answer to how Coltrane continually improvised masterpiece after masterpiece?

A: My best answer, honestly, is that he practiced. He was an obsessive–he practiced obsessively, even after a gig. He would play a gig and then go back to his hotel room and practice. And he was, I think, obsessed with an idea that was well beyond a performance, well beyond what a critic or a listener thought. He was really after some sort of musical perfection: the ability to have an idea that he had never had before, have that idea be profound and, at the same time, be able to execute that idea. That's a remarkable trio of goals to have right there. I think he knew that the only way he would even come close was to keep that horn in his mouth.

About the Author

Alicia Anstead is editor in chief of the national magazine Inside Arts *for the Association of Performing Arts Presenters in Washington, D.C., and is a contributing editor to Harvard Arts Beat, a blog for Harvard University's Office for the Arts.*

Section 2: Music and Learning

2.1 Music Lessons Combat Poverty's Effect on the Brain
By Simon Makin

2.2 Hearing the Music, Honing the Mind
By The Editors

2.3 Music Helps Kids Read
By Jenni Laidman

2.4 Rhythm and Music Help Math Students
By Sophie Bushwick

2.5 Does Music Boost Your Cognitive Performance?
By Cindi May

2.6 Everyone Can Gain from Making Music
By Julia Calderone

2.7 Fact or Fiction?: Babies Exposed to Classical Music End Up Smarter
By Nikhil Swaminathan

2.8 Math, Music and Imagination
By Marcus Miller

2.9 You Don't Have to Start Young to Be a Great Musician
By Cindi May

2.10 Even A Few Years Of Music Training Benefits The Brain
By Christie Wilcox

2.11 Speaking in Tones: Music and Language Partner in the Brain
By Diana Deutsch

Music Lessons Combat Poverty's Effect on the Brain

By Simon Makin

Scientists have observed that reading ability scales with socioeconomic status. Yet music might help close the gap, according to Nina Kraus and her colleagues at Northwestern University.

Kraus's team tested the auditory abilities of teenagers aged 14 or 15, grouped by socioeconomic status (as indexed by their mother's level of education, a commonly used surrogate measure). The researchers recorded the kids' brain waves with EEG as they listened to a repeated syllable against soft background sound and when they heard nothing. They found that children of mothers with a lower education had noisier, weaker, and more variable neural activity in response to sound and greater activity in the absence of sound. The children also scored lower on tests of reading and working memory.

Kraus thinks music training is worth investigating as a possible intervention for such auditory deficits. The brains of trained musicians differ from nonmusicians, and they also enjoy a range of auditory advantages, including better speech perception in noise, according to research from Kraus's laboratory. The researchers admit that this finding could be the result of preexisting differences that predispose some people to choose music as a career or hobby, but they point out that some experimental studies show that musical training, whether via one-on-one lessons or in group sessions, enhances people's response to speech.

Most recently Kraus's group has shown that these effects may last. Kraus surveyed 44 adults aged 55 to 76 and found that four or more years of musical training in childhood was linked to faster neural responses to speech, even for the older adults who had not picked up an instrument for more than 40 years.

About the Author

Simon Makin is a freelance science journalist based in the U.K. His work has appeared in New Scientist, *the* Economist, Scientific American *and* Nature, *among others. He covers the life sciences and specializes in neuroscience, psychology and mental health.*

Hearing the Music, Honing the Mind

By The Editors

Nearly 20 years ago a small study advanced the notion that listening to Mozart's *Sonata for Two Pianos in D Major* could boost mental functioning. It was not long before trademarked "Mozart effect" products appealed to neurotic parents aiming to put toddlers on the fast track to the Ivy League. Georgia's governor even proposed giving every newborn there a classical CD or cassette.

The evidence for Mozart therapy turned out to be flimsy, perhaps nonexistent, although the original study never claimed anything more than a temporary and limited effect. In recent years, however, neuroscientists have examined the benefits of a concerted effort to study and practice music, as opposed to playing a Mozart CD or a computer-based "brain fitness" game once in a while. Advanced monitoring techniques have enabled scientists to see what happens inside your head when you listen to your mother and actually practice the violin for an hour every afternoon. And they have found that music lessons can produce profound and lasting changes that enhance the general ability to learn. These results should disabuse public officials of the idea that music classes are a mere frill, ripe for discarding in the budget crises that constantly beset public schools.

Studies have shown that assiduous instrument training from an early age can help the brain to process sounds better, making it easier to stay focused when absorbing other subjects, from literature to tensor calculus. The musically adept are better able to concentrate on a biology lesson despite the racket in the classroom or, a few years later, to finish a call with a client when a colleague in the next cubicle starts screaming at an underling. They can attend to several things at once in the mental scratch pad called working memory, an essential skill in this era of multitasking.

Discerning subtleties in pitch and timing can also help children or adults in learning a new language. The current craze for high school Mandarin classes furnishes an ideal example. The difference between *m ¯a* (a high, level tone) and *mà* (falling tone) represents the difference between "mother" and "scold." Musicians, studies show, are better than nonmusicians at picking out easily when your *m ¯a* is *mà*ing you to practice. These skills may also help the learning disabled improve speech comprehension.

Sadly, fewer schools are giving students an opportunity to learn an instrument. In *Nature Reviews Neuroscience* this summer, Nina Kraus of Northwestern University and Bharath Chandrasekaran of the University of Texas at Austin, who research how music affects the brain, point to a disturbing trend of a decline of music education as part of the standard curriculum. A report by the advocacy organization Music for All Foundation found that from 1999 to 2004 the number of students taking music programs in California public schools dropped by 50 percent.

Research of our brains on music leads to the conclusion that music education needs to be preserved—and revamped, as needed, when further insights demonstrate, say, how the concentration mustered to play the clarinet or the oboe can help a problem student focus better in math class. The main reason for playing an instrument, of course, will always be the sheer joy of blowing a horn or banging out chords. But we should also be working to incorporate into the curriculum our new knowledge of music's beneficial effect on the developing brain. Sustained involvement with an instrument from an early age is an achievable goal even with tight budgets. Music is not just an "extra."

Music Helps Kids Read

By Jenni Laidman

She probably didn't realize it, but your preschool teacher very likely provided your first reading lesson when she cranked up "Yellow Submarine" and handed you a noisemaker. Today a symphony of research trumpets the many links among language, reading, and music, including several that reveal a connection between rhythm and reading skills. Nina Kraus of Northwestern University has discovered a possible explanation: the brains of good beat keepers respond to speech more consistently than the brains of people whose toes do not tap in time. After testing 124 adolescents for beat-keeping ability, the researchers used an electroencephalogram (EEG) to eavesdrop on teen brains as the consonant sound "da" was played repeatedly. With every "da," the brains of beat keepers responded consistently, even when there was background noise or while they watched television. The brain waves of poor beat keepers, however, were all over the place.

The study helps to explain why music may hold a key to improved reading. Because reading ability, in general, relies on making a connection between the sounds of letters and symbols on a page, music provides another avenue into learning. "Through music, you learn to pay attention to important sounds," Kraus says. The inconsistent sound processing shown by the poor beat keepers makes that difficult. "If you have an auditory system that automatically is able to efficiently pull out sounds that are meaningful, it's going to be important not just for music but for speech.

Rhythm and Music Help Math Students

By Sophie Bushwick

Stuck on a tricky math problem? Start clapping. Grade school kids who learned about fractions through a rhythm-and-music-based curriculum outperformed their peers in traditional math classes. The work is in *Educational Studies in Mathematics*. [Susan Joan Courey et al., "Academic music: music instruction to engage third-grade students in learning basic fraction concepts"]

Fractions let you divide up a measure of music into notes of varying length. For example, one four-beat measure could contain a single whole note held for all four beats, two half notes of two beats apiece, four quarter notes of a beat each, and so on. In the Academic Music program, based on the Kodaly method of musical education, students clap, drum and chant to memorize the lengths of musical notes–then solve problems in which fractional notes must add up to a full measure of music.

Sixty-seven students participated in the study. Half did math problems using the Academic Music system. And after six weeks, the students in the music program averaged 50 percent higher on tests than did the kids in regular math class. Fractions create a solid foundation for further math education–so mastering them is music to educators' ears.

–*Sophie Bushwick*

[The above text is a transcript of this podcast.]

Does Music Boost Your Cognitive Performance?

By Cindi May

Music makes life better in so many ways. It elevates mood, reduces stress, and eases pain. Music is heart-healthy, because it can lower blood pressure, reduce heart rate, and decrease stress hormones in the blood. It also connects us with others and enhances social bonds. Music can even improve workout endurance and increase our enjoyment of challenging activities.

The fact that music can make a difficult task more tolerable may be why students often choose to listen to it while doing their homework or studying for exams. But is listening to music the smart choice for students who want to optimize their learning?

A new study by Manuel Gonzalez of Baruch College and John Aiello of Rutgers University suggests that for some students, listening to music is indeed a wise strategy, but for others, it is not. The effect of music on cognitive functioning appears not to be "one-size-fits-all" but to instead depend, in part, on your personality–specifically, on your need for external stimulation. People with a high requirement for such stimulation tend to get bored easily and to seek out external input. Those individuals often do *worse*, paradoxically, when listening to music while engaging in a mental task. People with a low need for external stimulation, on the other hand, tend to improve their mental performance with music.

But other factors play a role as well. Gonzalez and Aiello took a fairly sophisticated approach to understanding the influence of music on intellectual performance, assessing not only listener personality but also manipulating the difficulty of the task and the complexity of the music. Whether students experience a perk or a penalty from music depends on the interplay of the personality of the learner, the mental task, and the music.

In the study, participants first completed the Boredom Proneness Scale, which is a personality test used to determine need for external stimulation. They then engaged in an easy cognitive task (searching for the letter A in lists of words) and a more challenging one (remembering word pairs). To control for practice and fatigue effects, half of the subjects completed the easy task first, while the other half completed the challenging one first. Participants finished both tasks under one of three sound conditions: (a) no music, (b) simple music, or (c) complex music. All of the music was instrumental, and music complexity was manipulated by varying the number of instruments involved in the piece. Simple music included piano, strings, and synthesizer, while complex music added drums and bass to the simple piece.

The data suggest that your decision to turn music on (or off) while studying should depend on your personality. For those with a high need of external stimulation, listening to music while learning is not wise, especially if the task is hard and/or the music is complex. On the simple task of finding As, such subjects' scores for the music condition were the same (for simple music), or significantly worse (for complex music) than those for the silent condition. On the complex task of learning word pairs, their performance was worse whenever music was played, regardless of whether it was simple or complex.

For those with a low need of external stimulation, however, listening to music is generally the optimal choice. On the simple task of finding As, such participants' scores for the music condition were the same (for simple music) or dramatically *better* (for complex music) than those for the silent condition. On the complex task of learning word pairs, the participants showed a small but reliable benefit with both simple and complex music, relative to silence.

The results suggest that there are substantial individual differences in the impact of music on cognitive function, and thus recommendations regarding its presence in the classroom, study hall, or work environment may need to be personalized. Students who are easily bored and who seek out stimulation should be wary of adding music to the mix, especially complex music that may capture attention and consume critical cognitive resources that are needed for successful task completion. On the other hand, students with a low need for stimulation may benefit significantly from the presence of music, especially when completing simple, mundane tasks.

Before students decide to slip in their earbuds, though, they should carefully consider both their musical selection and the nature of the task. All of the music used in the present study was instrumental, and lyrical music will likely be more complex. Complexity appears to increase arousal, and the Yerkes-Dodson law suggests that a moderate level of arousal produces optimal performance. When there is too little or too much arousal, performance drops. Thus, the benefits of music for those with a low need for external stimulation that were observed here could diminish or even disappear with the added complexity of lyrics.

Similarly, increases in the complexity of a cognitive task might also reduce or eliminate the benefit of music. Although the "complex" task used in this study (learning word pairs) was only moderately challenging, the increase in complexity, relative to the simple task, was enough to reduce music's positive effect. With a highly challenging cognitive task (e.g., text comprehension or exam preparation), even those with a low need for external stimulation may fail to show such an effect with music.

With the right (low-need-for-stimulation) personality, the right (instrumental) music and the right (low-to-moderately-difficult) task, the presence of music may significantly improve cognitive functioning. Given the many other physical, emotional, and psychological benefits of music, that subscription to Spotify just might pay for itself!

About the Author

Cindi May is a professor of psychology at the College of Charleston. She explores avenues for improving cognitive function and outcomes in college students, older adults and individuals who are neurodiverse.

Everyone Can Gain from Making Music

By Julia Calderone

Think back to your elementary school music class. You absorbed commands from a baton-wielding conductor while deciphering inky notes on a page. You kept tempo with the rest of the band while your contorted fingers sped from key to key. There is no doubt that musical training is a challenge for the brain. And in the past decade an abundance of studies have found that this effort confers cognitive benefits on all who study music, from toddlers to retirees.

Researchers became interested in the effects of music on the brain when a provocative study in the early 1990s claimed that simply listening to a Mozart sonata could make you brainier–so dubbed the "Mozart effect." The finding was never confirmed. Various studies followed that showed listening to music has transient effects on cognitive functions such as spatial ability, speed of processing and creative problem solving–but such effects last only about 10 minutes once the music is switched off. Experts continue to debate wheth,er frequently engaging with music has longer-term effects on cognition. In recent years new techniques to measure the brain's response to auditory cues in real time have given researchers valuable data to address the issue. "We can see how these ingredients of sound are processed by the brain," says Nina Kraus, an auditory neuroscientist at the Northwestern University School of Communication. Today some evidence suggests that musical training may enhance a suite of cognitive functions, including listening, linguistics, focus, and memory, along with spatial, motor, and mathematical skills.

Better Reading Through Music

Young children are ripe subjects for research in this field because their brains are primed to develop language skills, which music seems to enhance. Many studies suggest that children who are musically trained have stronger cognitive abilities, including better vocabulary, reading skills, and sound perception. Yet these studies leave unanswered the important question of correlation: Are musicians better at certain tasks because of musical practice alone? Or are they drawn to music because they have these skills already or because they come from advantaged backgrounds?

Kraus and her colleagues have conducted a number of studies to tackle this question. In one experiment published last September, they gathered 44 children aged six to nine from disadvantaged schools in Los Angeles and asked them to participate in musical instruction for two hours a week. One group practiced for one year; the other practiced for two. After administering a battery of neurophysiological tests that recorded their brain activity, Kraus's team found that those who participated in the music program for two years, independent of their age, were markedly better at processing speech syllables–such as differentiating between the sounds [ba] and [ga]–than those who had only one year of training.

As Kraus explains, a key element of literacy is the ability to discern meaningful differences between speech sounds–so studying music, which shares characteristics with speech such as pitch, timing, and timbre, may help kids read better. The authors say the study provides the first direct evidence that a community music program for at-risk youth has a biological effect on the children's developing nervous systems. Other experts urge caution when interpreting these results. "We already know that music training makes you a better listener," says psychologist Glenn Schellenberg, who researches music's effect on cognition at the University of Toronto Mississauga. Until researchers have behavioral evidence that kids who get music training become superior at reading or perceiving speech, he explains, the question of whether music can influence language development remains open.

Empathetic Multitaskers

As a musician grows up, other cognitive benefits appear, among them a better ability to multitask, according to a 2014 study by psychologist

Melody Wiseheart and her colleagues at York University in Toronto. The team recruited 153 university students aged 18 to 31, about half of whom were musicians with about 12 years of formal musical training; the others were nonmusicians. The students performed multitasking exercises, such as switching between identifying how many numbers were on a screen and indicating which particular number was on the screen or tracking a moving white dot with their mouse while monitoring a flashing set of letters.

"We found that musicians were doing a lot better," Wiseheart says; they were about 30 percent more accurate than the nonmusicians when performing two tasks at once. She says that musicianship appears to enhance working memory, which underlies the ability to multitask and can boost skills both in and out of the classroom–when holding numbers in mind to compute an equation, for instance, or avoiding distractions while driving.

Playing in a band or singing in a choir provides another type of benefit important for this age group. Studies show that making music in a group improves communication, coordination, cooperation, and empathy among group members. Many of these advantages of musicianship may be felt for decades, but some may not. For example, child musicians appear to have better spatial reasoning than their nonmusician peers, but adult musicians do not.

Preventing Age-Related Decline

Many areas in which child and young adult musicians outperform their nonmusician peers–such as processing speed, memory, and attention–also happen to correlate with areas of cognitive decline in old age. A small but growing body of evidence suggests that lifelong musical practice makes our brains healthier as we age–especially in combating hearing loss, which affects an estimated two thirds of adults older than 70 in the U.S. A series of studies by neuroscientist Alexandra Parbery-Clark of the Swedish Medical Center in Seattle and her colleagues found that musicians aged 45 to 65 appear to lack four of the five hallmark declines of speech processing in old age–

they maintained consistent and speedy brain responses to speech, for example, and the ability to understand speech in noisy settings.

In addition, studies suggest that older adult musicians tend to have stronger memory, more focused attention, and faster brain processing. Although such effects are most evident in adults who have practiced their instrument at least twice a week for 20 minutes a session since childhood, researchers think that such benefits may also exist for less enthusiastic hobbyists. The act of making music appears to be key because it requires the integration of various senses, motor coordination, and concentration in a way that even very attentive listening does not.

What this means is that learning to play a musical instrument is very good for you. And when that practice begins early in life, its positive effects can stretch into old age. "Biologically, our past shapes our present," Kraus says. Both she and Wiseheart hope educators and policy makers will take note of this research and keep music in classrooms. As Kraus says, "We want to improve human communication by harnessing the brain's ability to change."

About the Author

Julia Calderone is a freelance science writer based in New York City.

Fact or Fiction?: Babies Exposed to Classical Music End Up Smarter

By Nikhil Swaminathan

The phrase "Mozart effect" conjures an image of a pregnant woman who, sporting headphones over her belly, is convinced that playing classical music to her unborn child will improve the tyke's intelligence. But is there science to back up this idea, which has spawned a cottage industry of books, CDs, and videos?

A short paper published in *Nature* in 1993 unwittingly introduced the supposed Mozart effect to the masses. Psychologist Frances Rauscher's study involved 36 college kids who listened to either 10 minutes of a Mozart sonata in D-major, a relaxation track, or silence before performing several spatial reasoning tasks. In one test–determining what a paper folded several times over and then cut might look like when unfolded–students who had listened to Mozart seemed to show significant improvement in their performance (by about eight to nine spatial IQ points).

Rauscher–whose work, unlike that of most scientists, is sometimes cited on the liner notes of CDs–remains puzzled as to how this narrow effect of classical music extended from a paper-folding task to general intelligence and from college students to children (and fetuses). "I think parents are very desperate to give their own children every single enhancement that they can," she surmises.

In addition to a flood of commercial products in the wake of the finding, in 1998 then-Georgia governor Zell Miller mandated that mothers of newborns in the state be given classical music CDs. And in Florida, day-care centers were required to pipe symphonies through their sound systems.

A 2004 Stanford study tracked the media's coverage of Rauscher's study relative to other studies published in *Nature* around the same period. In the U.S.'s top 50 newspapers, her paper, titled "Musical and Spatial Task Performance," was cited 8.3 times more often than the second-most popular paper (co-authored by famed astronomer Carl Sagan).

"It seems to be a circumscribed manifestation of a widespread, older belief that has been labeled 'infant determinism,' the idea that a critical period early in development has irreversible consequences for the rest of a child's life," the researchers wrote in their analysis. "It is also anchored in older beliefs in the beneficial powers of music."

Some still argue for such musical powers. "Music has a tremendous organizing quality to the brain," notes Don Campbell, a classical musician who has written more than 20 books on music, health and education, including *The Mozart Effect®* and *The Mozart Effect® for Children*. Referencing French physician Alfred Tomatis's work in music therapy on children with dyslexia, attention-deficit disorders, and autism in the mid-20th century, he believes music that's not highly emotional or overly rhythmic has a multilayered influence on the individual, from modulating mood to alleviating stress. "I know it improves our ability to be intelligent," he adds.

But in 1999 psychologist Christopher Chabris, now at Union College in Schenectady, N.Y., performed a meta-analysis on 16 studies related to the Mozart effect to survey its overall effectiveness. "The effect is only one and a half IQ points, and it's only confined to this paper-folding task," Chabris says. He notes that the improvement could simply be a result of the natural variability a person experiences between two test sittings.

Earlier this year, the Federal Ministry of Education and Research in Germany published a second review study from a cross-disciplinary team of musically inclined scientists who declared the phenomenon nonexistent. "I would simply say that there is no compelling evidence that children who listen to classical music are going to have any improvement in cognitive abilities," adds Rauscher, now an associate professor of psychology at the University of Wisconsin–Oshkosh. "It's really a myth, in my humble opinion."

Rather than passively listening to music, Rauscher advocates putting an instrument into the hands of a youngster to raise intelligence. She cites a 1997 University of California, Los Angeles, study that found, among 25,000 students, those who had spent time involved in a musical pursuit tested higher on SATs and reading proficiency exams than those with no instruction in music.

Despite its rejection by the scientific community, companies like Baby Genius continue to peddle classical music to parents of children who can purportedly listen their way to greater smarts.

Chabris says the real danger isn't in this questionable marketing, but in parents shirking roles they are evolutionarily meant to serve. "It takes away from other kinds of interaction that might be beneficial for children," such as playing with them and keeping them engaged via social activity. That is the key to a truly intelligent child, not the symphonies of a long-dead Austrian composer.

Math, Music, and Imagination

By Marcus Miller

Like most New Yorkers, I tend to work late. My typical evening involves leaving the stage shortly after midnight and then preparing some problems in number theory or combinatorics until about 3 or 4 a.m. I am a jazz musician and mathematician. My skill set allows me to interpret musical experience through the language of mathematical structure and creative problem solving.

My practice involves using ideas of mathematical transformations on melodies, rhythms, and harmony. My compositions are developed using relationships between sound frequencies. But, to me, the notion that math and music are the same thing is both terribly poetic and also too reductionist to be useful. Still I believe the two disciplines are connected by an uncanny similarity in the roles creativity and imagination play in both.

I started learning music at nine years old and worked as a musician through my teenage years, but opted to attend a university instead of a conservatory on the advice of my music mentors who encouraged me to learn more about the world. At school, I became enamored of math because of the allure of the elegant theoretical worlds mathematicians built. Upon graduation, however, I decided to spend my 20s back on stage rather than in a graduate school library. Still, I continued reading math texts, as well as tutoring high school and college students, whenever I wasn't touring around the world.

The uses of math in music are legion. You can find math the construction of modern harmony and counterpoint, development of rhythms, and the proportioning of arrangements. What I would like to see further explored, are the commonalities between the subjective experiences of doing math and music. Although the lifestyles of mathematicians and musicians might seem worlds apart, at least for me, the "thought work" behind them are more closely related than you might think: the magic of engaging with math and music fundamentally changes the way you imagine and create.

Much of this "thought work" can be summarized as first *creating*, in the senses (and perhaps on a whiteboard or an instrument), a representation of an idea, and then *imagining* it transformed in creative and useful ways. Developing the representation is thus a form of self discovery, while transforming it is a kind of play. Can you spot the inference to be made here? It deeply informs my life and I would love to see it become more present in our culture: *Math can be experienced as play in much the same way music is.*

Let me explain. To improvise or compose one must learn the technique of the instrument and the harmonic and rhythmic language of music. All the while, the fun comes in imagining and experimenting with the technical and linguistic components one has incorporated, in order to invoke a sensation, express an emotion, or tell a story. As the mastery of both the instrument and the underlying language expand, the mind becomes more sensitive to different ideas while the body becomes more competent at putting those ideas in practice. The process thus expands naturally from creative absorption to transformation, and eventually to execution.

Math can work similarly. A student must become adept with numbers and other symbols, various rules of algebra and calculus to manipulate symbols, and several functions. This is the language of mathematics; its grammar, and its technique. Mathematical problems can be viewed as structured opportunities to play with what is already known in order to discover what is not.

Through this process, a mathematician begins to develop a sense of the nature of mathematical ideas and their logical interrelationships, thus becoming sensitive to new ideas while becoming better equipped to manipulate them internally. To think of math as just formulas memorized through rote learning and mechanical thoughtless symbol shunting tragically misses the point.

As with music, everyone incorporates the underlying language, grammar, and technique in their senses differently, and thus comes to their own individual understanding that leads them to express ideas in their own unique way. Contrary to the trope of the socially dysfunctional lone genius, mathematicians collaborate for most of their work, which makes them in some sense much like musicians. Expressing our internal worlds through pictures, words, and symbols and sharing them with one another, riffing off of each other's ideas is how much of modern mathematics is done.

What if the world understood math in this way? What if we educated with the idea of playing with numbers in order to master arithmetic the same way improvising musicians are taught to play with musical notes to learn their scales? What if we honored the unique way that people understand and taught from that space rather than by rote? What if we refined people's logical aesthetics to the point that mathematics felt more personal, more artsy, and the profound experiences of mathematical "beauty," "elegance" or "risk" weren't reserved for an intellectual elite?

Math as self-discovery, math as play. These two ideas may seem foreign at first, but I am convinced this change in paradigm is exactly what's needed in order to enlarge the tribe of creative problem solvers in mathematics and many other human disciplines–equipping them to "jam" on the world's toughest challenges.

The views expressed are those of the author(s) and are not necessarily those of Scientific American.

About the Author

Marcus Miller is a mathematician and a jazz musician based in New York.

You Don't Have to Start Young to Be a Great Musician

By Cindi May

Wolfgang Amadeus Mozart began his musical training at the tender age of three. By age five, he had already composed his first piece of music. As a child, he mastered the piano, along with several other instruments including the violin, organ, and harpsichord. By all accounts, he was a child prodigy. But he was far from the only composer to have a head start: Ludwig van Beethoven, Martha Argerich, Vincenzo Bellini, Claudio Arrau, and many of history's greatest musicians all began their training in early childhood and went on to wow the world.

The success of these musicians raises the question: Do you need to start early to be great? Many of us assume that the younger we start, the better our chances of becoming the best. Certain research backs up this claim. Some psychologists have even suggested that there may be a key period in early childhood when we have a particularly powerful capacity to absorb musical aptitude. According to this view, if you wait until your teens or even early adulthood to begin your training, you will have missed a critical window.

Yet a new study by Laura Wesseldijk of Vrije University Amsterdam and her colleagues challenges this view: It explores the possibility that environmental and familial factors are the driving forces behind the success of "early starters." Such individuals may have an edge not because they learn in a developmentally unique period but because they inherit talent, have access to instruments and instruction, or get a head start on practice. So it is possible that starting late might not prevent you from becoming great.

When comparing early starters to late bloomers, one critical factor to consider is total practice time. We know that practice matters because it can take thousands of hours to achieve expertise. Any study seeking to isolate the benefits of early exposure has to match training time for those who start early versus late in life. But there is a challenge in matching total training time: late bloomers with extensive practice tend to be much older than early starters with the same practice. Given that some kinds of cognitive performance often start to decline in early adulthood, comparing old late bloomers to young early starters could inflate the advantages of beginning young.

To add to the challenge, practice time and age are not the only factors to consider. Imagine you are the child of a concert pianist. It is possible that some aspects of musical talent have a genetic component, and if so, you may have inherited a predisposition to excel musically. Even if you did not, you are raised in a musically-enriched environment, with a piano in your home and a parent who plays regularly. Either your natural talent or your experience, or both, may lead you to begin banging on the piano keys as a toddler. Lucky for you, you have a parent with the knowledge and expertise to nurture that interest. You are indeed an early starter, but you also have familial and environmental advantages that could accelerate your musical development.

Wesseldijk and her colleagues explored the effect of these familial and environmental influences by assessing musical aptitude and expertise in two independent populations–professional musicians and adult twins with musical experience. By including professional musicians, the researchers assessed aptitude and expertise in a cohort of highly trained, active experts who had begun their training at varying ages (from age two to 18). Through studying identical twins, the researchers could examine differences in aptitude and expertise for pairs of individuals who shared the same familial environment and genetic predispositions but may have started their training at different times.

More than 300 musicians and 7,000 twins participated in the study, and they ranged in age from 27 to 54. The musicians selected were still active in the field, and each of the twins had received musical training at some point in their lives. Participants reported the age at which they started to play and the hours they practiced each week during different age intervals (for example, six to 11 years and 12 to 17 years). Using this information, the researchers estimated the age of onset of training and accumulated practice for each participant. Participants also completed two online assessments: one for musical aptitude and the other for musical achievement. The aptitude test measured the basic musical skills of pitch, melody, and rhythm discrimination. The achievement test evaluated different metrics of musical success, including the body of composed and performed works, number of awards, national and international reviews, and pieces featured in public performances.

The team's findings suggest that early starters do not benefit from a critical developmental window for cultivating skill and expertise but rather from additional hours of practice, the experience of growing up in a musically engaged family, and perhaps even a genetic predisposition for musical prowess. They first examined the relation between starting early and later musical aptitude and achievement in both the musician and twin samples, controlling for total practice time. In this analysis, an earlier start in musical training was associated with higher scores on some aptitude measures but not higher musical achievement. In other words, when total practice was held constant, individuals who were exposed to music at an early age showed higher scores on the basic skill of pitch discrimination–yet they were no more likely than late bloomers to have their music played on the radio or in public concerts, to win awards, or to receive national or international reviews.

To understand the contribution that genes and environment play in musical prowess, researchers turned to the twin data. Researchers estimated genetic and environmental factors by comparing identical twins to each other, to fraternal twins (who share only 50 percent of their genes on average), and to experienced musicians in the general population. If there is no genetic component to musical talent, then the data from identical twin pairs should be similar to data from fraternal twin pairs. Similarly, if familial environment has no influence on musical success, then data for twins reared together should look the same as data for unrelated musicians. Not surprisingly, the findings suggest that heredity and environment do contribute to musical aptitude and achievement. When the researchers further controlled for these genetic and environmental influences, an early start was no longer predictive of musical aptitude. Put simply: the early starters didn't score higher on the aptitude tests because they began their training earlier but because of genetic and environmental factors that gave them an edge. Children who have a natural talent for music and/or a musically gifted parent are more likely to be exposed to music at an early age and have their talent nurtured. These factors explain the advantage that early starters have over late bloomers with respect to musical skill.

So we can all take a breath and relax if we (or our children) failed to start playing a musical instrument by the age of five. You didn't miss the window because, as the findings demonstrate, no such window exists. If your passion for the piano emerges in your teens or even in adulthood, you are not destined for mediocrity. Those of us learning to play later in life can still aspire to greatness, just as Bill Withers, who began his musical career in his late 20s, still managed to write and produce award-winning music and to be inducted into the Rock and Roll Hall of Fame. That said, one essential ingredient in the recipe for success is practice. If you don't get an early start, you may need to stay up late, putting in the hours—practice makes perfect.

About the Author

Cindi May is a professor of psychology at the College of Charleston. She explores avenues for improving cognitive function and outcomes in college students, older adults and individuals who are neurodiverse.

Even A Few Years Of Music Training Benefits The Brain

By Christie Wilcox

Music has a remarkable ability to affect and manipulate how we feel. Simply listening to songs we like stimulates the brain's reward system, creating feelings of pleasure and comfort. But music goes beyond our hearts to our minds, shaping how we think. Scientific evidence suggests that even a little music training when we're young can shape how brains develop, improving the ability to differentiate sounds and speech.

With education funding constantly on the rocks and tough economic times tightening many parents' budgets, students often end up with only a few years of music education. Studies to date have focused on neurological benefits of sustained music training, and found many upsides. For example, researchers have found that musicians are better able to process foreign languages because of their ability to hear differences in pitch, and have incredible abilities to detect speech in noise. But what about the kids who only get sparse musical tutelage? Does picking up an instrument for a few years have any benefits?

The answer from a study just published in the *Journal of Neuroscience* is a resounding yes. The team of researchers from Northwestern University's Auditory Neuroscience Laboratory tested the responses of 45 adults to different complex sounds ranging in pitch. The adults were grouped based on how much music training they had as children, either having no experience, one to five years of training, or six to eleven years of music instruction.

Music training had a profound impact on the way the study subjects' brains responded to sounds. The people who had studied music, even if only for a few years, had more robust neural processing of the different test sounds. Most importantly, though, the adults with music training were more effective at pulling out the fundamental frequency, or lowest frequency sound, of the test noises.

"The way you hear sound today is dictated by the experiences with sound you've had up until today," explained co-author and lab head Nina Kraus. As she and her colleague wrote in an article for Nature, "akin to physical exercise and its impact on body fitness, music is a resource that tones the brain for auditory fitness."

Bulking up the auditory brain has non-musical implications. The ability to differentiate fundamental frequencies is critical for perceiving speech, and is an integral part of how we recognize and process sounds in complex and noisy environments. Thus childhood music instruction has strong linguistic benefits and improves performance on everyday listening tasks. Since we live in an inherently noisy world, the better we are at focusing on sound and perceiving different sounds, the better. This can be particularly important for children with learning disorders or those for whom English is a second language.

There is a body of research that suggests music training not only improves hearing, it bolsters a suite of brain functions. Musically trained kids do better in school, with stronger reading skills, increased math abilities, and higher general intelligence scores. Music even seems to improve social development, as people believe music helps them be better team players and have higher self-esteem. "Based on what we already know about the ways that music helps shape the brain, the study suggests that short-term music lessons may enhance lifelong listening and learning," said Kraus. "Our research captures a much larger section of the population with implications for educational policy makers and the development of auditory training programs that can generate long-lasting positive outcomes."

The importance of music education is something to consider, given that election season is in full swing. According to a recent White House report, more than 300,000 education jobs have been lost since the "end" of the recession in 2009 - 7,000 were lost last month alone. As schools lose funding, arts and extracurricular programs are often first on the chopping block, meaning less music education for the nation's youth. Given the scientific evidence supporting the importance of music both neurologically and educationally, the loss of music education seems particularly painful. Perhaps as we head to the polls this season, we should give even more thought as to how our choices of elected officials might affect the education system in this country and the brains of the children who are its future.

Referenced

Skoe, E. & Kraus, N. (2012). A Little Goes a Long Way: How the Adult Brain Is Shaped by Musical Training in *Childhood, Journal of Neuroscience*, 32 (34) 11510. DOI: 10.1523/JNEUROSCI.1949-12.2012

The views expressed are those of the author(s) and are not necessarily those of Scientific American.

About the Author

Christie Wilcox is a postdoctoral researcher in cellular and molecular biology at the University of Hawaii, where she studies venom. She is also a science blogger and communicator.

Speaking in Tones: Music and Language Partner in the Brain

By Diana Deutsch

One afternoon in the summer of 1995, a curious incident occurred. I was fine-tuning my spoken commentary on a CD I was preparing about music and the brain. To detect glitches in the recording, I was looping phrases so that I could hear them over and over. At one point, when I was alone in the room, I put one of the phrases, "sometimes behave so strangely," on a loop, began working on something else and forgot about it. Suddenly it seemed to me that a strange woman was singing! After glancing around and finding nobody there, I realized that I was hearing my own voice repetitively producing this phrase—but now, instead of hearing speech, I perceived a melody spilling out of the loudspeaker. My speech had morphed into song by the simple process of repetition.

This striking perceptual transformation, which I later found occurs for most people, shows that the boundary between speech and song can be very fragile. Composers have taken account of the strong connections between music and speech, for example, incorporating spoken words and phrases into their compositions. In addition, numerous vocalizations seem to fall near the boundary between speech and song, including religious chants and incantations, oratory, opera recitative (a style of delivery in opera resembling sung ordinary speech), the cries of street vendors, and some rap music.

And yet for decades the experience of musicians and the casual observer has clashed with scientific opinion, which has held that separate areas of the brain govern speech and music. Psychologists, linguists, and neuroscientists have recently changed their tune, however, as sophisticated neuroimaging techniques have helped amass evidence that the brain areas governing music and language overlap. The latest data show that the two are in fact so intertwined that an awareness of music is critical to a baby's language development and even helps to cement the bond between infant and mother. As children grow older, musical training may foster their communication skills and even their reading abilities, some studies suggest. What is more, the neurological ties between music and language go both ways: a person's native tongue influences the way he or she perceives music. The same succession of notes may sound different depending on the language the listener learned growing up, and speakers of tonal languages such as Mandarin are much more likely than Westerners to have perfect pitch.

Word Symphonies

Musicians and philosophers have long argued that speech and melody are interconnected. Russian composer Modest Mussorgsky believed that music and talk were in essence so similar that a composer could reproduce a conversation. He wrote to his friend Rimsky-Korsakov: "Whatever speech I hear, no matter who is speaking ... my brain immediately sets to working out a musical exposition of this speech." Indeed, when you listen to some of his piano and orchestral works, you may suddenly find that you are "hearing" the Russian language.

Despite such informal evidence of the ties between speech and music, researchers—bolstered in part by patients whose brain damage affected their speech but spared their musical ability—began espousing the opposite view around the middle of the 20th century. The brain divides into two hemispheres, and these experts hypothesized that its functions were just as neatly organized, with language residing on the left side and music on the right. Their theory was that the neural signal for dialogue bypassed the usual pathways for sound processing and instead was analyzed in an independent "module" in the brain's left hemisphere. That module supposedly excluded nonverbal sounds such as music. Similarly, the theory went, music was processed in a right-hemisphere module that excluded speech sounds. This attractive dichotomy became so popular that it effectively shut out for decades any thought that language and music might be neurologically—and functionally—intertwined.

But then, by the late 1990s, a generation of young researchers who did not have a stake in the separation of speech and song began questioning the idea. They brought to light existing data indicating that some aspects of music engage the left hemisphere more than the right. In addition, pioneering new experiments, many of which were conducted with emerging technology such as functional magnetic resonance imaging, showed that music and speech are not as neurologically separate as researchers had supposed.

One line of investigation demonstrated that the perception and appreciation of music could impinge on brain regions classically regarded as language processors. In a 2002 study neuroscientist Stefan Koelsch, then at the Max Planck Institute for Human Cognitive and Brain Sciences in Leipzig, Germany, and his colleagues presented participants with sequences of chords while using functional MRI to monitor their brains. They found that this task prompted activity on both sides of the brain but most notably in two regions in the left hemisphere, Broca's and Wernicke's areas, that are vital for language processing and that many researchers had assumed were solely dedicated to this function. Other more recent studies have revealed that speaking activates many of the same brain regions as analogous tasks that require singing. These and dozens of findings by other experimenters have established that the neural networks dedicated to speech and song significantly overlap.

This overlap makes sense, because language and music have a lot in common. They are both governed by a grammar, in which basic elements are organized hierarchically into sequences according to established rules. In language, words combine to form phrases, which join to form larger phrases, which in turn combine to make sentences. Similarly, in music, notes combine to form phrases, which connect to form larger phrases, and so on. Thus, to understand either language or music, listeners must infer the structure of the passages that they hear, using rules they have assimilated through experience.

In addition, speech has a natural melody called prosody. Prosody encompasses overall pitch level and pitch range, pitch contour (the pattern of rises and falls in pitch), loudness variation, rhythm, and tempo. Prosodic characteristics often reflect the speaker's emotional state. When people are happy or excited, they frequently speak more rapidly, at higher pitches and in wider pitch ranges; when people are sad, they tend to talk more slowly, in a lower voice and with less pitch variation. Prosody also helps us to understand the flow and meaning of speech. Boundaries between phrases are generally marked by pauses, and the endings of phrases tend to be distinguished by lower pitches and slower speech. Moreover, important words are often spoken at higher pitches. Interestingly, some pitch and timing characteristics of spoken language also occur in music, which indicates that overlapping neural circuitries may be involved.

Meaningful Melodies

At birth, babies are already familiar with the melody of their mother's speech. Audio recordings taken from inside the womb at the beginning of labor reveal that speech sounds produced by the mother can be loudly heard. The phrases reaching the baby have been filtered through the mother's tissues, however, so that the crisp, high frequencies–which carry much of the information important for identifying the meanings of words–are muted, whereas the musical characteristics of speech–its pitch contours, loudness variations, tempo, and rhythmic patterning–are well preserved.

These spoken melodies seem to set the stage for mother-child bonding. In an ingenious experiment published in 1980, psychologists Anthony J. DeCasper of the University of North Carolina at Greensboro and William P. Fifer, now at Columbia University, recorded new mothers reading a story out loud. In this experimental setup, the newborn babies could turn on the recordings by sucking on a pacifier, a connection they learned over time, and they sucked more frequently when their actions produced their mothers' voices compared with those of other women. The researchers reasoned that the newborns preferred to listen to the voices with which they had become familiar before birth. Then, in 1996, psychologists Melanie J. Spence and Mark S. Freeman of the University of Texas at Dallas reported carrying out a similar experiment in which they used a low-pass filter to muffle recorded female voices so that they sounded as they would in the womb. The newborn babies preferred their mothers' filtered voices over those of other women, again indicating that they had become familiar with the melodies of their mothers' utterances in the womb.

In addition to forging a nascent connection between mother and child, early exposure to musical speech sounds may begin the process of learning to talk. In one 1993 study, for example, two-day-old babies preferred to listen to recordings of speech in their native language to those in a foreign tongue. Because such young babies could only have become familiar with such speech in the womb, the results suggest that the babies initially become comfortable with the musical qualities of their language.

Accordingly, music may be the first part of speech that babies learn to reproduce; infants echo the inherent melodies of their native language when they cry, long before they can utter actual words. In a study published in 2009 medical anthropologist Kathleen Wermke of the University of Wrzburg in Germany and her colleagues recorded the wails of newborn babies–which first rise and then fall in pitch–who had been born into either French- or German-speaking families. The researchers found that the cries of the French babies consisted mostly of the rising portion, whereas the descending segment predominated in the German babies' cries. Rising pitches are particularly common in French speech, whereas falling pitches predominate in German. So the newborns in this study were incorporating into their cries some of the musical elements of the speech to which they had been exposed in the womb, showing that they had already learned to use some of the characteristics of their first language.

After birth, the melody of speech is also vital to communication between mother and infant. When parents speak to their babies, they use exaggerated speech patterns termed motherese that are characterized by high pitches, large pitch ranges, slow tempi, long pauses and short phrases. These melodious exaggerations help babies who cannot yet comprehend word meanings grasp their mothers' intentions. For example, mothers use falling pitch contours to soothe a distressed baby and rising pitch contours to attract the baby's attention. To express approval or praise, they utter steep rising and falling pitch contours, as in "Go-o-o-d girl!" When they express disapproval, as in "Don't do that!" they speak in a low, staccato voice.

In 1993 psychologist Anne Fernald of Stanford University reported exposing five-month-old infants from English-speaking families to approval and prohibition phrases spoken in German, Italian and nonsense English, as well as regular English motherese. Even though all this speech was gibberish to the babies, they responded with the appropriate emotion, smiling when they heard approvals and becoming subdued or crying when they heard prohibitions. Thus, the melody of the speech alone, apart from any content, conveys the message.

Although the ability to detect speech melodies is inborn, people can hone this skill by taking music lessons. In a study published in 2009 neuroscientists Mireille Besson of CNRS in France and Sylvain Moreno, now at the Rotman Research Institute in Toronto, and their colleagues recruited eight-year-old children who had been given no musical training and divided them into two groups. One group took music lessons for six months while the other enrolled in painting lessons. Before and after this training, the children listened to recorded sentences; in some of these, the last word was raised in pitch so that it sounded out of keeping with the rest of the sentence, and the children were asked to detect the altered sentences. At the start, the two groups did not differ in their ability to detect the pitch changes, but after the six months of instruction, the children who had taken music lessons outperformed the others.

Musically trained children may thus be at an advantage in grasping the emotional content–and meaning–of speech.

Musical training may affect perception of prosody in part by tuning the auditory brain stem–a group of structures that receive signals from the ear and help to decode the sounds of both speech and music. In a 2007 investigation neuroscientists Patrick Wong and Nina Kraus, along with their colleagues at Northwestern University, exposed English speakers to Mandarin speech sounds and measured the electrical responses in the auditory brain stem using electrodes placed on the scalp. The responses to Mandarin were stronger among participants who had received musical training–and the earlier they had begun training and the longer they had continued training, the stronger the activity in these brain areas.

Additional research shows that music lessons can improve the ability to detect emotions conveyed in speech (presumably through a heightened awareness of prosody). In a study published in 2004 psychologist William F. Thompson and his colleagues at the University of Toronto gave a group of six-year-old children musical keyboard lessons for a year and then tested their ability to identify emotions expressed in spoken sentences, comparing their scores with those of children who did not receive musical training. They found that the kids who received music lessons were better at identifying whether sentences were spoken in a fearful or angry tone of voice–even when the sentences were spoken in an unfamiliar language.

Musical training might even accelerate the process of learning to read. Good readers tend to do better than poor readers on tests of musical ability (although there are many exceptions to this rule). In their 2009 study Moreno and his colleagues found that the eight-year-olds who had taken music lessons also showed better reading ability than the children who had instead learned to paint, suggesting that facility with music may spill over into skill at deciphering the written word. Researchers have even suggested that musical training (in combination with other therapies) might be useful in remedying dyslexia.

Talking in Tune

Not only can exposure to music enhance our language skills, but the speech we hear also influences our perception of music. For example, in a musical illusion called the tritone paradox, which I discovered in the 1980s, a listener hears two computer-generated tones that are half an octave (or tritone) apart, one after the other. Each tone is a clearly defined note such as C, C-sharp or D, but its octave is inherently ambiguous so that a note could be, say, middle C, an octave above or below middle C, or any other C. The listener then decides whether the pattern ascends or descends in pitch. (Because of the ambiguity in the octave placement of the notes, there is no correct answer, and perception varies by listener.) Interestingly, I found that such judgments depend on the language or dialect to which the listener has been exposed. For example, in a 1991 study I asked people who had been raised in California and those raised in the south of England to judge these tritones and found that when the Californians tended to hear the pattern as ascending, the southern English subjects tended to hear it as descending, and vice versa. In another study published in 2004 my colleagues and I found the same dichotomy between listeners from Vietnam and native English speakers born in California, suggesting that the language we learn early in life provides a musical template that influences our perception of pitch.

Such a template might also constrain the pitch range of our speaking voice. In a study published in 2009 my colleagues and I examined the pitch ranges of female speech in two Chinese villages and found that these clustered together for people in the same village but differed across villages, suggesting that even local differences in the voices we hear around us can affect the pitch of the speech we produce.

The language to which we are exposed can also greatly influence the chances of developing perfect pitch–the ability to name the pitch of a note without a reference note. This skill is very rare in our culture: only an estimated one in 10,000 Americans have it. In

1997 I noticed that when I uttered a Vietnamese word without paying attention to its pitch, a native listener would either misunderstand me or have no idea what I was trying to say. But when I got the pitch right, the problem disappeared. Vietnamese and Mandarin are tone languages in which words take on entirely different meanings depending on the tones with which they are spoken. In Vietnamese, the word "ba" spoken in the mid-flat tone means "father;" the same word spoken in the low-descending tone means "grandmother." In Mandarin, the word "ma" means "mother" in a tone that is high and flat but "horse" in a tone that is low and first descends and then ascends.

I then learned that not only were Vietnamese and Mandarin speakers very sensitive to the pitches that they hear, but they can produce words at a consistent absolute pitch. In a study published in 2004 my colleagues and I asked native speakers of Mandarin and Vietnamese to recite a list of words in their native language on two separate days. We found that their pitches were remarkably consistent: when compared across days, half of the participants showed pitch differences of less than half a semitone. (A semitone is half a tone–that is, the difference between F and F-sharp.)

In light of these findings, I wondered if tone language speakers acquire perfect pitch for the tones of their language in infancy along with other features of their native tongue. Perfect pitch for musical tones would then be much easier for tone language speakers to develop than it would be for speakers of a nontone language, such as English. In an experiment published in 2006 my colleagues and I gave a test for perfect pitch to two large groups of music conservatory students–Mandarin speakers at the Central Conservatory of Music in Beijing and speakers of English or of another nontone language at Eastman School of Music in Rochester, N.Y.–and found that the prevalence of perfect pitch was indeed far higher among the Mandarin speakers. These findings were consistent with my hypothesis, but because the Central Conservatory students were all Chinese, the results could mean that genes that spur the development of perfect pitch are just more prevalent among Chinese people.

To decide which explanation was correct, my colleagues and I gave a test for perfect pitch to University of Southern California music conservatory students, including English speakers and three groups of East Asian students divided by how well they spoke their native tone language. Among the English speakers, the prevalence of perfect pitch was just 8 percent among those who had begun musical training at or before age five and 1 percent among those who had begun training between ages six and nine. The statistics were similar among the East Asian students who were not at all fluent in their native tone language. In contrast, the students who were very fluent tone language speakers performed extraordinarily well on our test: 92 percent of those who had begun musical training at or before age five had perfect pitch as did 67 percent of those who started music lessons between ages six and nine. The students who spoke a tone language moderately well fell between the two extremes. These findings, which we published in 2009, strongly indicate that the high prevalence of perfect pitch among the tone language speakers is not genetic but related to exposure to their language.

Thus, the language we learn in infancy, and continue to speak, can have a profound effect on the way in which we encode the sounds of music. Indeed, in many respects, music and speech seem to be mirror images, with both playing integral roles in the development of the other–in the way we, as people, bond and communicate, in how we perceive the sounds around us, in our understanding of language and in the workings of our minds.

Referenced

The Psychology of Music. Second edition. Edited by Diana Deutsch. Elsevier, 1999.

The Enigma of Absolute Pitch. Diana Deutsch in *Acoustics Today*, Vol. 2, pages 11–19; 2006.

Musicophilia: Tales of Music and the Brain. Oliver Sacks. Knopf, 2007.

Newborns' Cry Melody Is Shaped by Their Native Language. Birgit Mampe et al. in

Current Biology, Vol. 19, pages 1994–1997; 2009.

Perfect Pitch: Language Wins Out over Genetics. Diana Deutsch et al.: www.acoustics.org/press/157th/deutsch.html

The Speech-to-Song Illusion. Diana Deutsch et al.: www.acoustics.org/press/156th/deutsch.html

About the Author

Diana Deutsch is a professor of psychology at the University of California, San Diego, who studies the perception of music and language. She has recorded two CDs consisting of audio illusions that she has discovered: Musical Illusions and Paradoxes *and* Phantom Words and Other Curiosities *(http://philomel.com). In these anomalies, the perception of a given set of sounds varies among people or changes over time, even when the sounds remain the same. For examples, see http://deutsch.ucsd.edu.*

Section 3: The Healing Power of Music

3.1 "Alive Inside" Shows How Music Can Break Through the Fog of Dementia
By Annie Sneed

3.2 Heartbeat: Music May Help Keep Your Cardiovascular System in Tune
By Lynne Peeples

3.3 Music May Orchestrate Better Brain Connectivity in Preterm Infants
By Christopher Intagliata

3.4 How Music Can Literally Heal the Heart
By Elaine Chew, Psyche Loui, Grace Leslie, Caroline Palmer, Jonathan Berger, Edward W. Large, Nicolò F. Bernardi, Suzanne Hanser, Julian F. Thayer, Michael A. Casey, and Pier D. Lambiase

3.5 Music Can Heal the Brain
By William Forde Thompson and Gottfried Schlaug

"Alive Inside" Shows How Music Can Break Through the Fog of Dementia

By Annie Sneed

When asked about her childhood in the film *Alive Inside*, a 90-year-old woman with dementia replies, "I've forgotten so much, I'm very sorry." Filmmaker Michael Rossato-Bennett then plays music from her past for her. "That's Louis Armstrong," she says, "He's singing 'When the Saints Go Marching By' and it takes me back to my school days." She then proceeds to recall precise details from her life: that her mother told her not to listen to Louis Armstrong, the date of her birthday, that she worked at Fort Jackson during wartime, and much more.

Alive Inside documents the uncanny power of music to reawaken emotions and lost memories in people with dementia. Rossato-Bennett shadows Dan Cohen, a social worker and founder of the nonprofit Music & Memory, as he brings personalized music on iPods into nursing homes across the country. The transformation in emotion, awareness, and memory shown in these elderly patients may leave viewers incredulous, wondering "How is this possible?" A number of researchers have studied this topic, however, and they have some ideas about how music affects the brain–specifically, music that is deeply meaningful to the person.

Music tends to accompany events that arouse emotions or otherwise make strong impressions on us–such as weddings, graduations, and even spending good times with friends as a teenager. These kinds of experiences form strong memories, and the music and memories likely become intertwined in our neural networks, according to Julene Johnson, a professor at the University of California, San Francisco's Institute for Health and Aging. Movements, such as dancing, also often pair with our experience of music, which can facilitate memory formation. Even many years later, hearing the music can evoke memories of these long-past events.

As *Alive Inside* shows, music retains this power even for many people with dementia. Researchers note that the brain areas that process and remember music are typically less damaged by dementia than other regions, and they speculate that this sparing may explain the phenomenon.

Another contributing factor might be that elderly people with dementia, especially those in nursing homes, often live in an unfamiliar environment. "It's possible those long-term memories are still there," Johnson says, "but people just have a harder time accessing them because there's not a lot of context in which someone could pull out those memories." It seems that familiar music might be a good tool to provide context and reconnect with lost memories.

Johnson also notes that music will not have a strong effect on all people with dementia. "This isn't universal," she says. "There are some dementias where the recognition of music is impaired."

In addition to reawakening memories, research and anecdotes have shown that music can soothe agitated patients and thus may avoid the need for antipsychotic drugs to help them calm down.

Despite music's apparent benefits, few studies have explored its influence on memory recall in people with dementia. "It's really an untapped area," Johnson says. Petr Janata, a cognitive neuroscientist in the Center for Mind and Brain at the University of California, Davis, is one researcher investigating the topic of music and memory. He says that although scientists still do not have the answers for why and how music reawakens memories in people with dementia, there is tremendous anecdotal evidence that suggests it does work. "I don't think we're there yet with a bulletproof explanation for why this happens," Janata says, "but I do think this phenomenon is real and it's just a matter of time before it's fully borne out by scientific research."

In the meantime, though, Dan Cohen continues his mission of using music to help patients and their families and caregivers cope with dementia. "We need to use music to engage with people," Cohen says, "to allow them to express themselves, enjoy themselves and live again." And he is determined to make this happen all over the country—he has already brought iPods into 640 nursing homes and 45 states, and he aims to establish personalized music as a standard of care in all 50,000 care facilities in the U.S.

About the Author

Annie Sneed is a science journalist who has written for the New York Times, Wired, *Public Radio International and* Fast Company.

Heartbeat: Music May Help Keep Your Cardiovascular System in Tune

By Lynne Peeples

Music may calm the savage beast or, at least, make the workday seem shorter. A new study now adds cardiovascular health to the list of music's potential benefits, suggesting it can directly trigger physiological changes that modulate blood pressure, heart rate, and respiration.

"Music induces a continuous, dynamic–and to some extent predictable–change in the cardiovascular system," said Luciano Bernardi, a professor of medicine at the University of Pavia in Italy and lead author on the paper published in the journal *Circulation*, in a statement. Understanding the mechanisms of how swelling crescendos and deflating decrescendos affect our physiology, he suggests, could lead to potential new therapies for stroke and other conditions.

Bernardi and his colleagues had previously found that changes in the cardiovascular and respiratory systems mirrored musical tempo. To extend this knowledge to the body's response to changing rhythms, they enlisted 24 volunteers–half experienced singers, the remainder with no musical training.

While participants listened to five random selections of Beethoven, Bach, Puccini, and other classical artists as well as a two-minute segment of silence, monitors recorded physiological signals. The researchers found that selections with crescendos, especially those with a series of them (think: Queen's "Bohemian Rhapsody"), led to proportional constriction of blood vessels and increases in blood pressure, heart rate, and respiration. These measures decreased during decrescendos and silent periods. The team also found that "rich" music phrases around 10 seconds long, like those rhythms from famous arias by Verdi, caused heart rate and other parts of the cardiovascular system to synchronize with the music. Both groups experienced this entrainment, although the musicians showed a stronger response.

These results, Bernardi says, indicate that music's effects go beyond a patient's head. "It is not only the emotion that creates the cardiovascular changes," he notes, "but this study suggests that also the opposite might be possible." He believes the boosts in mood–including those pleasurable "chills"–triggered by music might also be a side effect of a physiological reaction.

Connie Tomaino, the executive director and co-founder of the Institute for Music and Neurological Function in New York City, has seen evidence of this mechanism in her own clinical practice. "The study hints at the possibility that some of these entrainment mechanisms act at the subconscious level," Tomaino says. "There's enough clinical evidence out there that shows this is true." She notes that even people in semivegetative states show respiratory changes when music is played.

Bernardi's study is limited by a small sample size and uniformity between participants–all were healthy Caucasians between the ages of 24 and 26. The authors suggest further research is needed to confirm and generalize their findings to the wider population and to other types of music.

Meanwhile, Tomaino finds Bernardi's study "really nicely supports previous inferences" into the science of music. (She is a consultant for a new documentary on PBS called "The Music Instinct: Science and Song," featuring an array of musicians including jazz, pop and rap and how they affect human mind and body.) She points to a paper published earlier this year that found a developing fetus is already equipped with the ability to distinguish changes in sound patterns, presumably in order to interpret and learn from the world around them. "We're prewired to be receptive to rhythm," Tomaino says. So, scaramouch, do the fandango.

About the Author

Lynne Peeples is a freelance science journalist based in Seattle.

Music May Orchestrate Better Brain Connectivity in Preterm Infants

By Christopher Intagliata

Fifteen million babies are born prematurely every year, worldwide. In some cases, the early births can be life-threatening or cause developmental issues.

"They have more attention-deficit difficulties. They can have a higher risk of having autism, and in general socio-emotional regulation issues." Petra Hüppi, a pediatrician and neonatologist at the University Hospital of Geneva.

Now, she and her colleagues have evidence that a simple tool could help those preterm babies' brains develop: music. But before you cue the Amadeus:

> "When I thought about Mozart, I thought, this is a very complex musical structure and I could hardly imagine that such an immature brain would be able to fully capture the complexity of Mozart."

So instead, she recruited the harpist Andreas Vollenweider, who worked with neonatal nurses to determine which sounds would most stimulate infants' brains. He then composed a suite of three eight-minute-long tracks, which the nurses played to 20 preterm babies using wireless headphones embedded in little baby caps. Each baby heard five tracks a week for six weeks on average.

Then Hüppi's team used MRIs to visualize activity in the babies' brains, and they found that preemies who listened to tunes had brain networks that more closely resembled those of full-term babies compared to their counterparts who didn't get the treatment. The music listeners had greater connectivity among brain regions, such as areas involved in sensory and higher-order cognitive functions—indicating that music listening might have enduring effects on brain development.

The details are in the *Proceedings of the National Academy of Sciences*.

Of course, many questions still remain. "How much should they listen to that? Was the music given in the right way? Would it be much better if it was something more lively than recorded music? Was it too simple? Could it be more complex?"

But Hüppi said one thing parents can already do is sing to their children. Plus, she said, it doesn't really matter if you can carry a tune.

–Christopher Intagliata

[The above text is a transcript of this podcast.]

How Music Can Literally Heal the Heart

By Elaine Chew, Psyche Loui, Grace Leslie, Caroline Palmer, Jonathan Berger, Edward W. Large, Nicolò F. Bernardi, Suzanne Hanser, Julian F. Thayer, Michael A. Casey, and Pier D. Lambiase

In a maverick method, nephrologist Michael Field taught medical students to decipher different heart murmurs through their stethoscopes, trills, grace notes, and decrescendos to describe the distinctive sounds of heart valves snapping closed, and blood ebbing through leaky valves in plumbing disorders of the heart.

Separately, in music based on electrocardiographic (ECG) traces of heart rhythm disorders, one of us–musician-mathematician Elaine Chew–used music notation to capture the signature rhythms of electrical anomalies of the heart. Collaged from extant music fragments matching the heartbeats, Brubeck's *Blue Rondo à la Turk* provided the 2:4:3 rhythmic tattoo of ventricular early beats, Piazzolla's *Le Grand Tango* remixed produced the irregular rhythms of atrial fibrillation. *Little Etudes for piano*, with pedagogical descriptions by cardiologist Pier Lambiase, provided a layperson's introduction to electrical aberrations of the heart.

The reason these heart-music mappings work is because abnormal heart rhythms tend to form simple inter-beat-interval ratios. In fact, the distinctive rhythms in Beethoven's music so closely resemble those of heart rhythm disorders that cardiologists have speculated that they may be transcriptions of Beethoven's possible arrhythmia, his interoceptive awareness of his own heartbeat enhanced by his deafness.

This is but one of multiple reasons music should be part of every heart physician's toolkit. Music and the heart have been romantically linked in popular consciousness due to their shared connections to human emotions and the brain. History is replete with examples of emotionally charged events followed almost immediately by the death of the person. The surgeon John Hunter famously pronounced, "My life is at the mercy of any scoundrel who should put me in a passion," before collapsing and dying after a heated board room meeting.

Cardiologists Peter Taggart and Pier Lambiase have been studying how emotions alter the conductive properties of individual heart cells. Mental stress changes the recovery period of heart cells after each heartbeat, called the action potential duration. Taggart co-authored a study in which patients whose hearts were paced at a steady rate watch the harrowing "cut the rope" scene from *Vertical Limit* (2000). The patients' action potential duration shortened under the stress. This may explain how more extreme stress coupled with underlying cardiac disease could precipitate life-threatening arrhythmias.

Acute stress produces dramatic effects in the heart, but slow-burning chronic stress due to protracted insecurity also predispose sufferers to disease and mortality. The sympathetic nervous system's default state of high alertness is suppressed when safety is perceived; these safety brakes are lifted under duress. The Generalized Unsafety Theory of Stress co-written by psychophysiologist Julian Thayer links the unconsciously perceived unsafety of prolonged stressors like low social status, early life adversity, or loneliness to hypervigilance that increases the odds of developing heart disease.

Music moves us in part because it draws on our primal intuitions about the heartbeat. Until the mid-19th century when it was replaced by the mechanical metronome, the human heartbeat provided the standard unit of measure for musical time. In his 1496 treatise, the *Practica Musicae*, the composer-theorist Franchinus Gaffurius wrote that the proper measure of the musical beat should be the pulse of a healthy human, noting that the pulses of "fevered persons" undergo an increase or become unequal in ways that worry physicians.

When we connect to the pulse of the music, we sense another's physiological states. The steady pulse at the beginning of Schubert's *Trio, Op. 100*, sets a strong but serene pace for its haunting melody. The breathless octaves in the opening of *Der Erlkrönig* evokes the rapid heart palpitations of the fevered boy in his father's arms, galloping through the stormy, windswept night. Hearing just heartbeats, pulse-only music, has been found to increase listeners' ability to sense what others are feeling in a study co-authored by musician-scientist Grace Leslie.

Music changes our heartrates, breathing, and blood pressure, and alters our heart rate variability, indicators of cardiac and mental health. Neuroscientist Psyche Loui and colleagues have traced music-induced physiological changes to a central node in the brain's networks, called the anterior insular, with dense connections to the vagus nerve, responsible for unconscious regulation of body functions.

The anterior insula is associated with empathetic mirroring of external and internal experiences. It is also connected to parts of the brain responsible for hearing (the auditory cortices) and for pleasure (the dopaminergic reward system). These auditory and reward network pathways likely subserve the mind's ability to form predictions and expectations during music listening. The systematic fulfilment and violation of expectations are thought to underlie emotion and meaning in music.

Music is an ideal catalyst for inducing physiological changes in heart-brain studies because it can be dissected systematically into features based on note content and the way this content is communicated in performance. Evidence suggests that these musical attributes trigger brain responses at a basic level. Analyzing listeners' brain imaging data in the OpenFMRI Study Forrest dataset, composer-neuroscientist Michael Casey found that specific music features induced predictable activation patterns in regions of listeners' brains. The activation patterns were consistent enough for machines to infer the music the listener heard or its genre simply from their fMRI scans.

Music features have also been linked to physiological responses. In a study co-authored by physicians Luciano Bernardi and Peter Sleight, loudness increases in vocal and orchestral music produced vascular constriction and blood pressure increases proportionate to these crescendos. Verdi arias with 10-second-long phrases–the period of Mayer waves, the body's natural blood pressure oscillation–

caused listeners' heart and respiratory signals to sync with the music envelop. Such unconscious physiological responses are thought to be the progenitors of music-induced emotions.

Music also has a communal impact on human physiology. People listening to the same music tend to synchronize not only their movements, but also their breathing and heart rhythms. Some of this heartbeat coherence is due to breathing together, but partial coherence (linear relationships) remained higher between the heartbeats of people vocalizing long notes together, over the baseline or breathing together, even after removing the effect of respiration.

The cognitive and physical demands of playing music also have measurable effects on musicians' heart rhythms and breathing patterns. Psychologists Caroline Palmer and Shannon Wright showed that repetitiveness of musicians' heart rhythms show greater rigidity (predictability) when playing unfamiliar musical melodies, and also when playing first thing after waking in the morning rather than in the evening.

For cardiac patients, music-based interventions can also modulate cerebral blood flow, reduce pre-operative anxiety and post-operative stress, improve surgery outcomes, and lower cortisol levels. Music interventions are found to significantly affect heartrate and blood pressure in coronary heart disease patients. Listening to relaxing music not only reduced heart and respiration rates but also oxygen demand of the heart in patients who have had a heart attack.

Technological advances in biofeedback sensors means that physiological parameters like heartbeats and heart rate variability can be harnessed to guide music interventions in cardiac therapy. Physiological feedback can be used to select or shape music to influence listeners' heart rates and breathing, for example, to increase heart rate variability. With widespread adoption of biofeedback devices, the tailoring of music interventions to individual cognitive or neural-cardiac states is now well within reach enabling a "musical prescription" for improved mental and physical wellbeing.

This is an opinion and analysis article; the views expressed by the author or authors are not necessarily those of Scientific American.

This article has been developed from an exploratory multidisciplinary seminar on Music and the Heart at the Radcliffe Institute for Advanced Study at Harvard University involving physicians, neuroscientists, and musicians with a specific interest in music and its effects on human physiology.

EC's and PDL's work is supported in part by the European Research Council (ERC) under the European Union's Horizon 2020 research and innovation programme (Grant agreement Nos. 788960 and 957532).

EL's work is supported in part by the National Science Foundation (NSF) under an NSF STTR Phase I Grant No. 2014870. Any opinions, findings and conclusions, or recommendations expressed in this material are those of the author(s), and do not necessarily reflect those of the funding agencies.

About the Authors

Elaine Chew, Ph.D., F.T.C.L., is a pianist-mathematician and principal investigator of the European Research Council–funded project COSMOS at the French National Center for Scientific Research (CNRS), where she is based at the Sciences and Technologies of Music and Sound Laboratory located at the Institute for Research and Coordination of Acoustics/Music (IRCAM).

Psyche Loui, Ph.D., is a neuroscientist-violinist and an associate professor and director of the Music, Imaging, and Neural Dynamics (MIND) Laboratory at Northeastern University.

Grace Leslie, Ph.D., a flutist, electronic musician and scientist, is an assistant professor of music technology at the Georgia Institute of Technology, where she directs the Brain Music Laboratory.

Caroline Palmer, F.R.S.C., is the Canada Research Chair in the Cognitive Neuroscience of Performance and a professor of psychology at McGill University, where she directs the Sequence Production Laboratory.

Jonathan Berger is the Denning Family Provostial Professor of Music and a Bass University Fellow in Undergraduate Education at Stanford University, and a composer-researcher at the Center for Computer Research in Music and Acoustics (CCRMA).

Edward W. Large, Ph.D., is director of the Music Dynamics Laboratory and the Theoretical Neuroscience Laboratory at the University of Connecticut, where he is a professor in the Department of Psychological Sciences and the Department of Physics.

Nicolò F. Bernardi, Ph.D., A.C.C., is a personal and professional coach and consultant who is trained as a cognitive neuroscientist, music therapist and yoga teacher.

Suzanne Hanser, Ed.D., is chair emerita and professor of music therapy at Berklee College of Music and president of the International Association for Music & Medicine.

Julian F. Thayer, Ph.D., a bassist and composer is the Distinguished University Professor in the Department of Psychological Science at the University of California, Irvine and Ohio Eminent Scholar Professor in Health Psychology Emeritus at the Ohio State University.

Michael A. Casey is a professor in the Department of Computer Science and the Department of Music at Dartmouth College.

Pier D. Lambiase is professor of cardiology at University College London Institute of Cardiovascular Science and Barts Heart Center and co-director of cardiovascular research at Barts Health NHS Trust.

Music Can Heal the Brain

By William Forde Thompson and Gottfried Schlaug

One day when Laurel was 11, she began to feel dizzy while playing with her twin sister and some friends in a park on Cape Cod. She sat down, and one of her friends asked her if she was OK. And then Laurel's memory went blank. A sudden blockage in a key blood vessel leading to the brain had caused a massive stroke. Blood could no longer reach regions crucial for language and communication, resulting in permanent damage. Laurel was still able to understand language, but she struggled to vocalize even a single word, and what she managed to say was often garbled or not what she had intended. Except when she *sang*.

Through a type of treatment called melodic intonation therapy, Laurel learned to draw on undamaged brain regions that moderate the rhythmic and tonal aspects of language, bypassing the speech pathways on the left side of her brain that were destroyed. In other words, she found her way back to language through music.

The therapeutic program that helped Laurel–like the others we focus on in our work as scientists and clinicians–is one of a new class of music-based treatments based directly on the biology of neurological impairment and recovery. These treatments aim to restore functions lost to injury or neurological disorders by enlisting healthy areas of the brain and sometimes even by reviving dysfunctional circuitry. As evidence accumulates about the effectiveness of these techniques, clinicians and therapists from a variety of fields have begun to incorporate them into their practices, most notably music therapists, who are at the intersection of music and health and important mediators of these interventions, as well as speech therapists and physical therapists. And among the beneficiaries are people diagnosed with stroke, autism, tinnitus, Parkinson's disease, and dementia.

As scientists learn more about the effect of music on cognitive and motor functions and mental states, they can tailor these therapies for each disorder, targeting specific brain injuries or dysfunctions. In Laurel's case, the treatments were designed to trigger, over time, the development of alternative neural pathways in healthy parts of the brain that would compensate for the lost pathways in the damaged language centers. But the ultimate aim was to help her recapture as much as she could of the world that had collapsed around her that day in the park.

Music as Medicine

Across cultures and throughout history, music listening and music making have played a role in treating disorders of the mind and body. Egyptian frescoes from the fourth millennium BCE appear to depict the use of music to enhance fertility in women. Shamans in the highland tropical forests of Peru use chanting as their primary tool for healing, and the Ashanti people of Ghana accompany healing ceremonies with drumming.

Much of the power of music-based treatment lies in its ability to meld numerous subtle benefits in a single, engaging package. Music is perhaps unrivaled by any other form of human expression in the range of its defining characteristics, from its melody and rhythm to its emotional and social nature. The treatments that take advantage of these attributes are rewarding, motivating, accessible, and inexpensive, and basically free of side effects, too. The attractive quality of music also encourages patients to continue therapy over many weeks and months, improving the chance of lasting gains.

The view that music can be useful in treating neurological impairment gained some scientific heft in a landmark study published in 2008. Psychologist Teppo Särkämö of the University of Helsinki and his team recruited 60 patients who had suffered a stroke in the middle cerebral artery of one hemisphere. They split the patients into three groups: the first participated in daily sessions of music listening, the second listened to audiobooks every day, and the third received no auditory treatment. Researchers observed the patients over two months. Those in the group that listened to music exhibited the greatest recovery in verbal memory and attention. And because listening to music appears to improve memory, the hope now is that active music making–singing, moving, and synchronizing to a beat–might help restore additional skills, including speech and motor functions in stroke patients.

The Singing Cure

The variety of music-based treatment that Laurel received springs from a remarkable observation about people who have had a stroke. When a stroke affects areas of the brain that control speech, it can leave patients with a condition known as nonfluent aphasia, or an inability to speak fluently. And yet, as therapists over the years have noted, people with nonfluent aphasia can sometimes sing words they cannot otherwise say.

In the 1970s neurologist Martin Albert and speech pathologists Robert Sparks and Nancy Helm (now Helm-Estabrooks), then at a Veterans Administration hospital in Boston, recognized the therapeutic implications of this ability and developed a treatment called melodic intonation therapy in which singing is a central element. During a typical session, patients will sing words and short phrases set to a simple melody while tapping out each syllable with their left hand. The melody usually involves two notes, perhaps separated by a minor third (such as the first two notes of "Greensleeves"). For example, patients might sing the phrase "How are you?" in a simple up-and-down pattern, with the stressed syllable ("are") assigned a higher pitch than the others. As the treatment progresses, the phrases get longer and the frequency of the vocalizations increases, perhaps from one syllable per second to two.

Each element of the treatment contributes to fluency by recruiting undamaged areas of the brain. The slow changes in the pitch of the voice engage areas associated with perception in the right hemisphere, which integrates sensory information over a longer interval than the left hemisphere does; as a consequence, it is particularly sensitive to slowly modulated sounds. The rhythmic tapping with the left hand, in turn, invokes a network in the right hemisphere that controls movements associated with the vocal apparatus. Benefits are often evident after even a single treatment session. But when performed intensively over months, melodic intonation therapy also produces long-term gains that appear to arise from changes in neural circuitry–the creation of alternative pathways or the strengthening of rudimentary ones in the brain. In effect, for patients with severe aphasia, singing trains structures and connections in the brain's right hemisphere to assume permanent responsibility for a task usually handled mostly by the left.

This theory has gained support in the past two decades from studies of stroke patients with nonfluent aphasia conducted by researchers around the world. In a study published in September 2014 by one of us (Schlaug) and his group at the Beth Israel Deaconess Medical Center and Harvard Medical School, 11 patients received melodic intonation therapy; nine received no treatment. The patients who received therapy were able to string together more than twice as many appropriate words per minute in response to a question. That same group also showed structural changes, assessed through MRI, in a right-hemisphere network associated with vocalization. The laboratory is now conducting studies to compare the benefits of melodic intonation therapy with other forms of therapy for patients with aphasia.

Because melodic intonation therapy seemed to work by engaging the right hemisphere, researchers then surmised that electrical or magnetic stimulation of the region might boost the therapy's power. In two recent studies that we conducted with our collaborators–one in 2011 at Beth Israel Deaconess and Harvard and the other in 2014 at the ARC Center of Excellence in Cognition and Its Disorders in Sydney, Australia–researchers stimulated an area in the right hemisphere called the inferior frontal gyrus, which helps to connect sounds with the oral, facial and vocal movements that produce them. For many participants, combining melodic intonation therapy with noninvasive brain stimulation yielded improvements in speech fluency after only a few sessions.

The benefits of melodic intonation therapy were dramatic for Laurel (who was part of a study led by Schlaug). The stroke had destroyed much of her left hemisphere, including a region crucial for language production known as Broca's area. When she began therapy in 2008, she could not string together more than two or three words, and her speech was often ungrammatical, leaving her frustrated whenever she tried to communicate. Her treatment plan was intensive–an hour and a half a day for up to five days a week, with 75 sessions in all. By the end of the 15-week treatment period, she could speak in sentences of five to eight words, sometimes more. Over the next several years she treated herself at home using the techniques she learned during the sessions. Today, eight years after her stroke, Laurel spends some of her time as a motivational speaker, giving hope and support to fellow stroke survivors. Her speech is not quite perfect but remarkable nonetheless for someone whose stroke damaged so much of her left brain. Evaluation of the long-term benefits of combination therapy is next on researchers' agenda.

Music and Motion

Music making can also help stroke survivors living with impaired motor skills. In a study published in 2007 neuropsychologist and music educator Sabine Schneider and neurologist Eckard Altenmueller, both then at the Hannover University of Music, Drama and Media in Germany, asked patients to use their movement-impaired hand to play melodies on the piano or tap out a rhythm on pitch-producing drum pads. Patients who engaged in this intervention, called music-supported training, showed greater improvement in the timing, precision, and smoothness of fine motor skills than did patients who relied on conventional therapy. The researchers postulated that the gains resulted from an increase in connections between neurons of the sensorimotor and auditory regions.

Rhythm is the key to treatment of people with Parkinson's, which affects roughly one in 100 older than 60. Parkinson's arises from degeneration of cells in the midbrain that feed dopamine to the basal ganglia, an area involved in the initiation and smoothness of movements. The dopamine shortage in the region results in motor problems ranging from tremors and stiffness to difficulties in timing the movements associated with walking, facial expressions, and speech.

Music with a strong beat can allay some of these symptoms by providing an audible rhythmic sequence that people can use to initiate and time their movements. Treatments include so-called rhythmic entrainment, which involves playing a stimulus like a metronome. In neurologist Oliver Sacks's 1973 book *Awakenings*, musical rhythm sometimes released individuals from their immobility, letting them dance or sing out unexpectedly.

The use of rhythm in motor therapy gained momentum in the 1990s, when musician, music therapist and neuroscientist Michael Thaut of Colorado State University and other researchers around the world demonstrated a technique called rhythmic auditory stimulation, or RAS, for people who had trouble walking, such as stroke and Parkinson's patients. A therapist will first ask patients to walk at a comfortable speed and then to an audible rhythm. Tempos that pushed patients slightly past their comfort zone yielded the greatest improvements in velocity, cadence, and stride length.

Despite these encouraging outcomes, the neural mechanisms that trigger improvements have been difficult to pin down. Imaging work suggests that during rhythmic auditory stimulation, neural control of motor behavior is rerouted around the basal ganglia; instead the brain stem serves as a relay station that sends auditory input to motor networks in the cerebellum, which governs coordination, and to other cortical regions that could help synchronize sound and motion.

Recovered Memory

Fewer neurological disorders inspire greater fear than dementia, one of the most common diseases of the elderly. According to some estimates, 44 million people worldwide are living with dementia, a number expected to reach 135 million by 2050. Alzheimer's disease, a neurodegenerative condition, accounts for more than 60 percent of the cases; multiple strokes can also cause so-called vascular dementia.

Music may be ideally suited to stimulating memory in people with dementia, helping them maintain a sense of self. Because music activates neural areas and pathways in several parts of the brain, the odds are greater that memories associated with music will survive disease. Music also stimulates normal emotional responses even in the face of general cognitive decline. In a 2009 study psychologist Lise Gagnon of the University of Sherbrooke in Quebec and her colleagues asked 12 individuals with Alzheimer's and 12 without it to judge the emotional connotations of various pieces of music. The Alzheimer's participants were just as accurate as the others despite significant impairments in different areas of judgment. Other research suggests that taking part in musical activities throughout life keeps the mind young and may even decrease the risk of developing dementia; the continuous engagement of the parts of the brain that integrate senses and motion with the systems for emotions and rewards might prevent loss of neurons and synapses.

The type of therapy that individual dementia patients receive will vary, from receptive (listening) to active (dancing, singing, clapping). Music that the patient selects is most effective because the choice represents a connection to memory and self. The benefits vary, too, and tend to be short-term. But when the treatment does work, it reduces the feelings of agitation that lead to wandering and vocal outbursts and encourages cooperation and interaction with others. Music therapy can also help patients with dementia sleep better and can enhance their emotional well-being.

These emotional and social benefits are clear in the case of June, an 89-year-old woman from New Hampshire. June has severe, irreversible dementia and is cared for at home by her daughter (who described her mother's circumstances to a clinician in Thompson's lab). Throughout the day, June is mainly nonresponsive and sits with her head hanging low. She cannot talk or walk, and she is incontinent. Yet when her daughter sings to her, June comes alive. She bangs her hands on her legs, smiles widely, and begins to laugh. June especially loves Christmas songs and may even blurt out a word or two. When listening to music, she can bang her leg in time with the beat.

Music on the Spectrum

Perhaps the most fascinating interplay between music and the brain lies in the case files of people with autism spectrum disorder, a neurodevelopmental syndrome that occurs in 1 to 2 percent of children, most of whom are boys. Hallmarks of autism include impaired social interactions, repetitive behaviors, and difficulties in communication. Indeed, up to 30 percent of people with autism cannot make the sounds of speech at all; many have limited vocabulary of any kind, including gesture.

One of the peculiarities of the neurobiology of autism is the overdevelopment of short-range brain connections. As an apparent consequence, children with autism tend to focus intensely on the fine details of sensory experience, such as the varying textures of different fabrics or the precise sound qualities emitted by appliances such as a refrigerator or an air conditioner. And this fascination with sound may account for the many anecdotal reports of children with autism who thoroughly enjoy making and learning music. A disproportionate number of children with autism spectrum disorder are musical savants, with extraordinary abilities in specialized areas, such as absolute pitch.

The positive response to music opens the way to treatments that can help children with autism engage in activities with other people, acquiring social, language, and motor skills as they do. Music also activates areas of the brain that relate to social ways of thinking. When we listen to music, we often get a sense of the emotional states of the people who created it and those who are playing it. By encouraging children with autism to imagine these emotions, therapists can help them learn to think about other people and what they might be feeling.

Recently the Music and Neuroimaging Laboratory at Beth Israel Deaconess and Harvard (which Schlaug directs) developed a new technique called auditory-motor mapping training, or AMMT, for children whose autism has left them unable to speak. The treatments have two main components: intonation of words and phrases (changing the melodic pitch of one's voice) and tapping alternately with each hand on pitch-producing drums while singing or speaking words and phrases. In a proof-of-principle study, six completely nonverbal children took part in 40 sessions of this training over eight weeks. By the end, all were able to produce some speech sounds, and some were even able to voice meaningful and appropriate words during tasks that the therapy sessions had not covered. Most important, the children were still able to demonstrate their new skills eight weeks after the training sessions ended.

Quiet, Please

Music-based treatments can also train the brain to tune out the phantom strains of tinnitus–the experience of noise or ringing in the ear in the absence of sound that affects roughly 20 percent of adults. Age-related hearing loss, exposure to loud sounds, and circulatory system disorders can all bring on the condition, with symptoms ranging from buzzing or hissing in the ears to a continuous tone with a definable pitch. The sensation can cause serious distress and interfere with the ability to concentrate on other sounds and activities. There is no cure.

The past decade has seen a surge in understanding of the neurological basis of the disorder. In one view, cochlear damage (most likely caused by exposure to loud sounds) reduces the transmission of particular sound frequencies to the brain. To compensate for the loss, neuronal activity in the central auditory system changes, creating neural "noise," perhaps by throwing off the balance between inhibition and excitation in the auditory cortex, leading to the perception of sounds that are not there. Also at play might be dysfunctional feedback to auditory brain regions from the limbic system, which is thought to serve as a noise-cancellation apparatus that identifies and inhibits irrelevant signals.

Music treatment seeks to counteract this dysfunction by inducing changes in the neural circuitry. For those with tonal tinnitus, one treatment involves listening to "notched music," generated by digitally removing the frequency band that matches the tinnitus frequency. The notching–pioneered and proved effective by neurophysiologist Christo Pantev and his group at the University of Münster in Germany–might help reverse the imbalance in the auditory cortex, strenghtening the inhibition of the frequency band that might be the source of the phantom sound in the first place. Another approach involves playing a series of pitches to patients and then asking them to imitate the sequence vocally. As the patients refine their accuracy, they learn to disregard irrelevant auditory signals and focus on what they want to hear. In time, the stimulus of effortful attention might help the auditory cortex return to its normal physiological state.

For any novel therapy, enthusiasm can sometimes outpace the evidence, and researchers have rightly pointed out that the new music-based treatments must prove their efficacy against the more established therapies. But of all the techniques for addressing neurological disorders, music-based therapies seem unique in their capacity to tap into emotions, to help the brain find lost memories, to let patients resume their place in the world. We are only now beginning to understand the science behind the belief in the power of music to heal.

Referenced

From Singing to Speaking: Why Singing May Lead to Recovery of Expressive Language Function in Patients with Broca's Aphasia. Gottfried Schlaug, Sarah Marchina and Andrea Norton in *Music Perception*, Vol. 25, No. 4, pages 315–323; April 1, 2008.

Listening to Tailor-Made Notched Music Reduces Tinnitus Loudness and Tinnitus-Related Auditory Cortex Activity. Hidehiko Okamota et al. in *Proceedings of the National Academy of Sciences USA*, Vol. 107, No. 3, pages 1207–1210; January 19, 2010.

Auditory-Motor Mapping Training as an Intervention to Facilitate Speech Output in Non-Verbal Children with Autism: A Proof of Concept Study. Catherine Y. Wan et al. in *PLOS ONE*, Vol. 6, No. 9, Article No. e25505; September 29, 2011.

Music, Health, and Wellbeing. Edited by Raymond MacDonald, Gunter Kreutz and Laura Mitchell. Oxford University Press, 2012.

Music, Thought, and Feeling: Understanding the Psychology of Music. Second edition. William Forde Thompson. Oxford University Press, 2014.

About the Authors

William Forde Thompson is a professor of psychology at Macquarie University in Sydney, Australia, and a chief investigator at the ARC Center of Excellence in Cognition and Its Disorders there.

Gottfried Schlaug is an associate professor of neurology at Harvard Medical School and Beth Israel Deaconess Medical Center and is a leading researcher on plasticity in brain disorders and music-based treatments for neurological impairments.

Section 4: Play It with Feeling: Music and Emotion

4.1 Let's Get Physical: The Psychology of Effective Workout Music
By Ferris Jabr

4.2 Why Does Music Make Us Feel?
By Mark Changizi

4.3 It's the Bass That Makes Us Boogie
By Karen Hopkin

4.4 Is a Sad Song Sad for Everyone?
By David Noonan

4.5 Dissecting the Bloodthirsty Bliss of Death Metal
By David Noonan

4.6 The Sound of Passion
By Patricia Moreau

4.7 Making Creepy Music Gives You Goose Bumps
By Amanda Baker

4.8 In Teen Music Choices, Anxiety Rules
By Abigail Baird

4.9 Why Music Moves Us
By Karen Schrock

Let's Get Physical: The Psychology of Effective Workout Music

By Ferris Jabr

I dare them to find the iPod on me," Richie Sais told the *New York Times* in 2007, when he was preparing to run the Marine Corps Marathon. USA Track & Field, the national governing body for distance racing, had just decided to ban athletes from using portable music players in order "to ensure safety and to prevent runners from having a competitive edge." Rais resolved to hide his iPod shuffle under his shirt. Many fellow runners protested the new rule, which remains in effect today in an amended form: It now applies only to people vying for awards and money.

For some athletes and for many people who run, jog, cycle, lift weights, and otherwise exercise, music is not superfluous–it is essential to peak performance and a satisfying workout. Although some people prefer audio books, podcasts, or ambient sounds, many others depend on bumpin' beats and stirring lyrics to keep themselves motivated when exercising. A quick Twitter search uncovers plenty of evidence: "Trying to let my phone charge a little more before I go, because lord knows I can't even try and workout without music," tweeted @Gianna_H21. "I just made my mom turn around to get my headphones. I can't possibly work out without music," @Codavoci_Kyle admitted.

In the last 10 years the body of research on workout music has swelled considerably, helping psychologists refine their ideas about why exercise and music are such an effective pairing for so many people as well as how music changes the body and mind during physical exertion. Music distracts people from pain and fatigue, elevates mood, increases endurance, reduces perceived effort, and may even promote metabolic efficiency. When listening to music, people run farther, bike longer, and swim faster than usual–often without realizing it. In a 2012 review of the research, Costas

Karageorghis of Brunel University in London, one of the world's leading experts on the psychology of exercise music, wrote that one could think of music as "a type of legal performance-enhancing drug."

Selecting the most effective workout music is not as simple as queuing up a series of fast, high-energy songs. One should also consider the memories, emotions, and associations that different songs evoke. For some people, the extent to which they identify with the singer's emotional state and viewpoint determines how motivated they feel. And, in some cases, the rhythms of the underlying melody may not be as important as the cadence of the lyrics. In recent years some researchers and companies have experimented with new ways to motivate exercisers through their ears, such as a smartphone app that guides the listener's escape from zombies in a postapocalyptic world and a device that selects songs based on a runner's heart rate.

Let Your Body Move to the Music

Research on the interplay of music and exercise dates to at least 1911, when American investigator Leonard Ayres found that cyclists pedaled faster while a band was playing than when it was silent. Since then psychologists have conducted around a hundred studies on the way music changes people's performance in a variety of physical activities, ranging in intensity from strolling to sprinting. Looking at the research as a whole, a few clear conclusions emerge.

Two of the most important qualities of workout music are tempo–or speed–and what psychologists call rhythm response, which is more or less how much a song makes you want to boogie. Most people have an instinct to synchronize their movements and expressions with music–to nod their heads, tap their toes or break out in dance–even if they repress that instinct in many situations. What type of music excites this instinct varies from culture to culture and from person to person. To make some broad generalizations, fast songs with strong beats are particularly stimulating, so they fill most people's workout playlists. In a recent survey of 184 college students, for example, the most popular types of exercise music were hip-hop (27.7 percent), rock (24 percent), and pop (20.3 percent).

Some psychologists have suggested that people have an innate preference for rhythms at a frequency of two hertz, which is equivalent to 120 beats per minute (bpm), or two beats per second. When asked to tap their fingers or walk, many people unconsciously settle into a rhythm of 120 bpm. And an analysis of more than 74,000 popular songs produced between 1960 and 1990 found that 120 bpm was the most prevalent pulse.

When running on a treadmill, however, most people seem to favor music around 160 bpm. Websites and smartphone apps such as Songza and jog.fm help people match the tempo of their workout music to their running pace, recommending songs as fast as 180 bpm for a seven-minute mile, for example. But the most recent research suggests that a ceiling effect occurs around 145 bpm: anything higher does not seem to contribute much additional motivation. On occasion, the speed and flow of the lyrics supersede the underlying beat: some people work out to rap songs, for example, with dense, swiftly spoken lyrics overlaid on a relatively mellow melody.

Although many people do not feel the need to run or move in exact time with their workout music, synchrony may help the body use energy more efficiently. When moving rhythmically to a beat, the body may not have to make as many adjustments to coordinated movements as it would without regular external cues. In a 2012 study by C. J. Bacon of Sheffield Hallam University, Karageorghis and their colleagues, participants who cycled in time to music required 7 percent less oxygen to do the same work as cyclists who did not synchronize their movements with background music. Music, it seems, can function as a metronome, helping someone maintain a steady pace, reducing false steps and decreasing energy expenditure.

Extending this logic, Shahriar Nirjon of the University of Virginia and his colleagues devised a personal music player that attempts to sync music with a runner's pace and heart rate. Accelerometers and a tiny microphone embedded in a pair of earbuds gauge the runner's pace and record the pulsing of blood vessels. The device wirelessly transmits the data it collects via a smartphone to a remote computer that chooses the next song.

Brain Beats

Recent research clarifies not only what type of music is best suited to a workout, but also how music encourages people to keep exercising. Distraction is one explanation. The human body is constantly monitoring itself. After a certain period of exercise—the exact duration varies from person to person—physical fatigue begins to set in. The body recognizes signs of extreme exertion—rising levels of lactate in the muscles, a thrumming heart, increased sweat production—and decides it needs a break. Music competes with this physiological feedback for the brain's conscious attention. Similarly, music often changes people's perception of their own effort throughout a workout: it seems easier to run those 10 miles or complete a few extra biceps curls when Beyoncé or Eminem is right there with you.

"Given that exercise is often tiresome, boring, and arduous, anything that relieves those negative feelings would be welcome," Karageorghis explains. The benefits of distraction are most pronounced during low- to moderate-intensity exercise. When up against high-intensity exercise, music loses its power to override the physical feelings of tiredness, but it can still change the way people respond to that fatigue. The right music elevates mood and persuades people to ride out waves of exhaustion, rather than giving up. Karageorghis cautions, though, against listening to music while running in heavily trafficked areas—distraction from fatigue is great, as long as it does not put you in danger.

Music also increases endurance by keeping people awash in strong emotions. Listening to music is often an incredibly pleasurable experience and certain songs open the mental floodgates with which people control their emotions in everyday situations. If one strongly identifies with the singer's emotions or perspective, the song becomes all the more motivational.

Consider a song from someone's favorite musical film or Broadway show, such as "One Day More" from *Les Misérables*—an ensemble song with a complex melody and building energy—or "Defying Gravity" from *Wicked*, in which Elphaba, a central character, vows to overcome all limits others have imposed on her. In addition to exhilarating melodies and vocals, such songs immediately recall the entire milieu of the performance and awaken memories of particular characters who are part of a complex narrative. This mesh of associations and connotations woven into the music provides not just a inspiring perspective to adopt, but also an entire alternate reality to enter while running in place on a treadmill at the gym. Some game designers have experimented with new ways for people to escape into fictional worlds while running. In 2012 the online game company Six to Start released the immersive running game, Zombies, Run!, in the form of a smartphone app that narrates the listener's quest to survive the zombie apocalypse. Following spoken prompts, the listener imagines him or herself running around to collect ammunition and medicine to complete various missions.

Whether music or zombie sound effects, what people listen to for motivation when they exercise acts on the same neural circuitry. "We are almost hardwired to appreciate music aesthetically," Karageorghis says. People's emotional response to music is visceral: It is, in part, ingrained in some of the oldest regions of the brain in terms of evolutionary history, rather than in the large wrinkly human cortex that evolved more recently. One patient—a woman known in the research literature as I. R.—exemplifies this primal response. I. R. has lesions to her auditory cortices, the regions of the cortex that process sound. When I. R. hears the normal version of a song and a horribly detuned version, she cannot tell the difference, explains Jessica Grahn, a cognitive neuroscientist who studies music at Western University's Brain and Mind Institute in Ontario. But when I. R. hears a happy song and a sad song, she immediately distinguishes them from one another.

Scientists now know that, although different regions of the human brain specialize in processing different senses—sound, sight, touch—the brain uses the information it receives from one sense to help it understand another. What people see and feel while listening to speech or music, for example, changes what they hear. Music and movement are particularly entangled in the brain. Recent studies suggest that—even if someone is sitting perfectly still—listening to enjoyable music increases electrical activity in various regions of the brain important for coordinating movements, including the supplementary motor area, cerebellum, basal ganglia, and ventral premotor cortex. Some researchers think that this neural crosstalk underlies people's instinct to move in time to music. "We have also known for decades that there are direct connections from auditory neurons to motor neurons," explains Grahn, who enjoys working out to cheesy techno-music. "When you hear a loud noise, you jump before you have even processed what it is. That's a reflex circuit, and it turns out that it can also be active for non-startling sounds, such as music."

In fact, the human brain may have evolved with the expectation that, wherever there is music, there is movement—although this idea emerges more from the imaginative minds of speculating evolutionary psychologists than from experimental evidence. Before the invention of reed flutes and other musical instruments, our ancestors likely produced the earliest forms of music by singing, screaming, chanting, or otherwise using their vocal cords, as well as by physically interacting with their own bodies, other people and the environment. A fast tempo would have likely required fast movements: quick clapping or foot stamping, perhaps. Deep, loud sounds would have demanded great energy and force—belting a note or beating the ground or a rock. In its conception, music was likely an extension of the human body. Maybe the brain remembers it that way.

About the Author

Ferris Jabr is a contributing writer for Scientific American. *He has also written for the* New York Times Magazine, *the* New Yorker *and* Outside.

Why Does Music Make Us Feel?

By Mark Changizi

As a young man I enjoyed listening to a particular series of French instructional programs. I didn't understand a word, but was nevertheless enthralled. Was it because the sounds of human speech are thrilling? Not really. Speech sounds alone, stripped of their meaning, don't inspire. We don't wake up to alarm clocks blaring German speech. We don't drive to work listening to native spoken Eskimo, and then switch it to the Bushmen Click station during the commercials. Speech sounds don't give us the chills, and they don't make us cry–not even French.

But music *does* emanate from our alarm clocks in the morning, and fill our cars, and give us chills, and make us cry. According to a recent paper by Nidhya Logeswaran and Joydeep Bhattacharya from the University of London, music even affects how we see visual images. In the experiment, 30 subjects were presented with a series of happy or sad musical excerpts. After listening to the snippets, the subjects were shown a photograph of a face. Some people were shown a happy face–the person was smiling–while others were exposed to a sad or neutral facial expression. The participants were then asked to rate the emotional content of the face on a seven-point scale, where one meant extremely sad and seven, extremely happy.

The researchers found that music powerfully influenced the emotional ratings of the faces. Happy music made happy faces seem even happier while sad music exaggerated the melancholy of a frown. A similar effect was also observed with neutral faces. The simple moral is that the emotions of music are "cross-modal," and can easily spread from sensory system to another. Now I never sit down to my wife's meals without first putting on a jolly Sousa march.

Although it probably seems obvious that music can evoke emotions, it is to this day not clear why. Why doesn't music feel like listening to speech sounds, or animal calls, or garbage disposals? Why is music *nice* to listen to? Why does music get blessed with a multi-billion dollar industry, whereas there is no market for "easy listening" speech sounds?

In an effort to answer, let's first ask why I was listening to French instructional programs in the first place. The truth is, I wasn't just listening. I was *watching* them on public television. What kept my attention was not the meaningless-to-me speech sounds (I was a slow learner), but the young French actress. Her hair, her smile, her mannerisms, her pout... I digress. The show was a pleasure to watch because of the *humans* it showed, especially the exhibited expressions and behaviors.

The lion share of emotionally evocative stimuli in the lives of our ancestors would have been from the faces and bodies of other people, and if one finds human artifacts that are highly evocative, it is a good hunch that it looks or sounds *human* in some way.

As evidence that humans are the principal source of emotionality among human artifacts, consider human visual signs. Visual signs, I have argued, have culturally evolved to look like natural objects, and have the kinds of contour combinations found in a three-dimensional world of opaque objects. Three-dimensional world of opaque objects? Nothing particularly human about that, and that's why most linguistic signs—like the letters and words on this page—are not emotionally evocative to look at.

But visual signs do *sometimes* have emotional associations. For example, colors are notoriously emotionally evocative, and arguments about what color something should be painted are the source of an alarming number of marital arguments. And "V" stimuli, such as that yield sign on the street, have long been realized (within the human factors literature) to serve as the most evocative geometrical shape for warning symbols. But notice that color and "V" stimuli are plausibly about human expression. In particular, color has recently been argued to be "about" human skin and the exhibited emotions—which is why red grabs our attention, since it's associated with blushing and blood—and "V" stimuli have been suggested to be "about" angry faces (namely, angry eyebrows).

Which brings us back to music and the Logeswaran paper. Music is exquisitely emotionally evocative, which is why a touch of happy music makes even unrelated pictures seem more pleasant. In light of the above, then, we are led to the conclusion that the artifact of music should contain some distinctly human elements.

The question, of course, is what those elements are. One candidate is our expressive speech—perhaps music is just an abstract form of language. However, most of the emotion of language is in the meaning, which is why foreign languages that we don't understand rarely make us swoon with pleasure or get angry. That's also why emotional speech from an unfamiliar language isn't featured on the radio!

But there is a second auditory expressive behavior we humans carry out—our bodily movements themselves. Human movement has been conjectured to underlie music as far back as the Greeks. As a hypothesis this has the advantage that we have auditory systems capable of making sense of the sounds of people moving in our midst —an angry stomper approaching, a delicate lilter passing, and so on. Some of these movements trigger positive emotions—they conjure up images of pleasant activities—while others might be automatically associated with fear or anxiety. (The sound of running makes us wonder what we're running from.) If music were speech-driven, then it is missing out on the largest part of speech's expressiveness—the meaning. But if music sounds like human expressive movements, then it sounds like something that, all by itself, is rich in emotional expressiveness, and can be easily interpreted by the auditory system.

Regardless of whether music is emotional intonation from speech or a summary of expressive movements—or something else altogether—the new research by Logeswaran and Bhattacharya adds yet more fuel to the expectation that music has been culturally selected to sound like an emotionally expressive human. While it is not easy for us to see the human ingredients in the modulations of pitch, intensity, tempo, and rhythm that make music, perhaps it is obvious to our auditory homunculus.

About the Author

Mark Changizi is a professor in the Department of Cognitive Science at Rensselaer Polytechnic Institute, and is the author of the recently published book The Vision Revolution.

It's the Bass That Makes Us Boogie

By Karen Hopkin

Karen Hopkin: This is *Scientific American*'s 60-Second Science. I'm Karen Hopkin.

Hopkin: Ever notice that some music just really makes you want to dance?

Well, a new study shows that it is, indeed, all about the bass. Because researchers have found that, during a concert, boosting the bass bumps up the boogying. The results appear in the journal *Current Biology.*

Daniel Cameron: Music and musical rhythm have been kind of fascinating to me for a long time, since I was a kid. In particular, the way that they make us feel.

Hopkin: Daniel Cameron is a postdoctoral fellow at McMaster University. He also plays drums.

Cameron: As a drummer, you're interested in making the crowd want to move and feel good and give a good pleasurable time feel. And this is related to the work I do in science.

Hopkin: Cameron and his colleagues want to understand how music can engender an almost irrepressible urge to feel our bodies in motion.

Cameron: And we knew from anecdotal evidence and other experimental evidence that there was an association between bass and dancing.

Hopkin: So, people who enjoy electronic dance music, or EDM, report that the thrumming bass produces a sensation that makes them want to move. And some studies have shown that our movements are more fine-tuned when we're locked onto bass notes.

Cameron: So, for example, if you have people tap along to a sequence of tones, their tapping is slightly more accurate, they're more synchronized...when those tones are low in frequency compared to high in frequency.

Hopkin: So the researchers set out to determine:

Cameron: If you add more bass to music, will it cause more dancing?

Hopkin: Now, they didn't want to manipulate the bass line in a way that was obvious. Because then people might consciously decide to step up their stepping out.

Cameron: That might be interesting...

Hopkin: But it would also muddy the results...like if someone in a drug trial knows they're getting the real deal and not a placebo.

Cameron: So we wanted to do a subtle manipulation, a very consciously undetectable manipulation.

Hopkin: So they broke out a set of very very low frequency speakers.

Cameron: These are specialized speakers. Kind of like sub-subwoofers. People might have subwoofers as part of their stereo system. And these are speakers that play even lower frequencies than most systems are able to do. Even lower frequencies than we think are typically able to be heard.

Hopkin: With their special speakers set up, the researchers staged a concert.

Cameron: We had the electronic music duo Orphx come to our LIVELab.

Hopkin: That's LIVE...L-I-V-E...for large, interactive virtual environment. It's like a cross between a performance space and a laboratory.

Cameron: The people who came to the show were fans of the group. They wanted to come and see EDM. They wanted to dance. And while they were there, we asked if they wanted to volunteer in our experiment. And a good number of people signed up.

Hopkin: Recruits adorned themselves with headbands bearing motion-capture reflectors...which the researchers used to track their movements.

Cameron: And then what we did was just, during the concert, turn these very low frequency speakers on, leave them on for two and a half minutes, turn them off. Leave them off for two and a half minutes. Back on for two and a half minutes. Off for two and a half minutes. On off on off. Throughout the concert.

Hopkin: Now, you can't hear when the speakers are switched on. And...based on the surveys filled out after the show...and a followup study of the manipulated audio clips...neither could the concert goers. But their feet sure knew something was up.

Cameron: What we found was, by looking at the motion capture data, people just moved more–they covered more ground, they moved faster–when the low frequency speakers were on. So this tells us that... the extra bass, these very very low frequencies, caused more moving.

Hopkin: About 12 percent more moving and grooving. So, the concert...and the experiment...were a success. Best of all...

Cameron: People enjoyed the concert. And...the more people moved, the more they enjoyed the concert.

Hopkin: Which shouldn't be a surprise.

Cameron: Dancing and pleasure really go hand in hand together. It's something we like to do with music, it's a pleasurable response, and we show with this work that bass is part of that mix.

Hopkin: Next up, Cameron says he'd like to look at whether bass can help bring us together.

Cameron: So people are more likely to feel good about one another and help one another if they've had some experience synchronizing their movements together. And dance is a great, fun way to do this. This might be related to why we find dance in all cultures and throughout history for the human species. It's a fundamental part of being human.

Hopkin: So, to cut down on conflict, maybe just crank up the bass and cut up the dance floor.

Hopkin: For *Scientific American*'s 60-Second Science, I'm Karen Hopkin.

[The above is a transcript of this podcast.]

About the Author

Karen Hopkin is a freelance science writer in Somerville, Mass. She holds a doctorate in biochemistry and is a contributor to Scientific American*'s 60-Second Science podcasts.*

Is a Sad Song Sad for Everyone?

By David Noonan

The ability of music to evoke specific, often powerful feelings is no secret to anyone who has listened to Gustav Mahler's Symphony No. 5, Billie Holiday's "God Bless the Child," the Ramones' "I Wanna Be Sedated," Lizzo's "Good as Hell," or any of the other countless compositions that have found their way onto Western playlists in the past few centuries.

The emotional effects of music are the point, of course. They are also the subject of a burgeoning field of research around the world in which scientists are exploring the nature of the many "subjective experiences"—such as joy, sadness, anxiety, and serenity—that music induces.

In a recent set of experiments, researchers at the University of California, Berkeley, and their colleagues sought to determine if the feelings that people experience when listening to music "show evidence of universality." They compared and analyzed how more than 2,800 U.S. and Chinese study participants responded to 2,168 (mostly Western) samples of instrumental music.

As it reports in a paper published this week in the *Proceedings of the National Academy of Sciences USA*, the team identified 13 distinct and very specific feelings that the Chinese and U.S. subjects shared when listening to music, despite their cultural differences.

The music used in the research, described in the paper as "the richest stimulus set of Western music samples ever studied," included classical, pop, rock, indie, hip-hop, R&B, country, film soundtracks, and more. An additional 189 samples of traditional Chinese music were also used. In all, the researchers gathered 375,230 judgments of the samples from the study participants.

In the first experiment, subjects listened to Western music samples (each of which was just five seconds long) and reported on the specific feelings they evoked, choosing responses from a list of 28 "categories of subjective experience" provided by the researchers.

Terms on the list included "triumphant/heroic," "sad/depressing," "joyful/cheerful," "awe-inspiring/amazing," and "dreamy." The team then used data-driven statistical modeling to identify the 13 shared experiences.

The second experiment, which included the Chinese music, involved broad evaluations of the samples by participants–such as whether the subjects liked or disliked them or found them exciting or not. A central finding of the study, the researchers write, is that specific feelings "drive the experience of music" more than the broader features. "When we hear a triumphant music sample, for example, somehow it unlocks this feeling of victory, of achievement," says Alan S. Cowen, a co-author of the paper and currently a visiting faculty researcher at Google. "We're thinking of something basic about the human experience."

Comparing Eastern and Western cultures is "a bit of a generalization," Cowen acknowledges. But "it does capture an axis along which people do vary." Differences in cultural norms and values noted in the paper include individualism in the U.S. versus collectivism in China and the relative importance of tradition in the two societies.

William Forde Thompson, a professor of psychology at Macquarie University in Australia and director of the school's Music, Sound and Performance Lab, wonders about the role played by the global influence of Western culture. "The novel finding here is that there is a lot of overlap in how Chinese and American participants assign emotional labels to music," says Thompson, who was not involved in the research. "This is important information, but it might be explained by the considerable overlap in exposure that participants have to Western media and the emotional vocabulary that is communicated by such media. It seems unlikely the overlap observed between American and Chinese listeners would be observed for all cultural groups, but that is an open question."

That concern is echoed by Samuel Mehr, head of the Music Lab at Harvard University. "The paper raises a lot of interesting questions about how music and emotion work," says Mehr, who also did not participate in the research. "This is a huge topic and one that we don't understand very well at all, but [this study] does a better job than any other paper I've seen on the topic at figuring out what emotions are there, at least in the music that they are studying. But I don't think we know at all how this generalizes to other forms of music, other cultures, and that sort of thing."

For their part, Cowen and his co-authors, including principal investigator Dacher Keltner of U.C. Berkeley, address the issue head-on in their paper. "In introducing quantitative approaches to study U.S. and Chinese experiences of music," they write, "we hope to set the stage for a broader project documenting shared and culture-specific understandings of music around the world. Different experiences may emerge when studying musical traditions from other regions, such as Africa and South America." Of particular interest, they note in the paper, will be the subjective experiences "associated with music in small-scale cultures with limited Western contact."

About the Author

David Noonan is a freelance writer specializing in science and medicine.

Dissecting the Bloodthirsty Bliss of Death Metal

By David Noonan

Brutality now becomes my appetite
Violence is now a way of life
The sledge my tool to torture
As it pounds down on your forehead

Shakespeare it's not. Those lyrics, from "Hammer Smashed Face" by the band Cannibal Corpse, are typical of death metal–a subgenre of heavy metal music that features images of extreme violence and the sonic equivalent of, well, a sledgehammer to the forehead.

The appeal of this marginal musical form, which clearly seems bent on assaulting the senses and violating even the lowest standards of taste, is mystifying to non-fans–which is one reason music psychologist William Forde Thompson was drawn to it. Thompson and his colleagues have published three papers about death metal and its fans this year, and several more are in the works.

"It's the paradox of enjoying a negative emotion that I was interested in," says Thompson, a professor at Macquarie University in Sydney, Australia. "Why are people interested in music that seems to induce a negative emotion, when in everyday life we tend to *avoid* situations that will induce a negative emotion?" A number of studies have explored the emotional appeal of sad music, Thompson notes. But relatively little research has examined the emotional effects of listening to music that is downright violent.

Thompson's work has produced some intriguing insights. The biggest surprise? "The ubiquitous stereotype of death metal fans–fans of music that contains violent themes and explicitly violent lyrics–[is] that they are angry people with violent tendencies," Thompson says. "What we are finding is that they are not angry people. They're not enjoying anger when they listen to the music, but they are in fact experiencing a range of *positive* emotions."

Those positive emotions, as reported by death metal fans in an online survey that Thompson and his team conducted, include feelings of empowerment, joy, peace, and transcendence. So far, almost all of the anger and tension Thompson has documented in his death metal studies has been expressed by non-fans after listening to samples of the music.

In a paper titled "Who enjoys listening to violent music and why?," published earlier this year in *Psychology of Popular Media Culture*, Thompson and colleagues sought to identify specific personality traits that distinguished death metal fans from non-fans. In the study, which involved 48 self-described death metal fans and 97 non-fans (all in their 20s), he deployed an arsenal of established psychological tools and measures. These included the Big Five Inventory (BFI) of personality–which assesses openness to experience, conscientiousness, agreeableness, and neuroticism–as well as the Interpersonal Reactivity Index (IRI), a 28-item measure of empathy.

Notably, on measures of conscientiousness and agreeableness, the scores of death metal fans were subtly but reliably lower than those of non-fans. One possible explanation for this finding, the authors write, "is that long-term, persistent exposure to violent media may lead to subtle changes in one's personality, desensitizing fans to violence and reinforcing negative social attitudes." But Thompson emphasizes that we just don't know. It is also possible that people with these personality traits are more likely to gravitate to death metal.

Results from the IRI showed the fan group and non-fan group with similar scores on the four dimensions of empathy that the index measures. When listening to death metal, however, study participants with lower empathy scores were more likely to experience higher levels of power and joy than those with greater empathic concern. That was true as well, Thompson found, for people whose personality assessment showed them to be more open to experience and less neurotic.

In the study, each participant listened to four out of eight 60-second samples of popular death metal songs (selected by the researchers from multiple online lists) and answered questions about the feelings the music evoked. The songs included "Slowly We Rot," by Obituary and "Waiting for the Screams," by Autopsy, as well as "Hammer Smashed Face."

In one set of responses, the subjects rated (on a scale of 1 to 7) the emotional effects of the music, using pre-selected terms such as "fear" and "wonder." In a second step, they described in their own words how death metal made them feel. "With its repetitive, fast-paced tempo, down-tuned instruments, and blast beats, it is virtually impossible not to be excited!" one fan wrote. "It sounds like messed-up teenagers making throaty, irritating noises about how bad their lives are," wrote a non-fan. "It's annoying."

The fact that the study relies on self-reporting by the subjects is a red flag for Craig Anderson, a psychology professor at Iowa State University who has spent his career researching the links between media violence and aggression, and who was not involved in Thompson's study. Self-reporting "may or may not reflect reality," Anderson says. "People may be lying to you, or, more likely, people don't have direct access to many of the kinds of effects that media have on them. They can construct an idea or hypothesis, and self-reports are essentially that kind of data. People may report that 'Oh yeah, this makes me feel this way,' without recognizing whether that's really true."

The paper acknowledges the limitations of self-reporting. But the researchers add that "the convergence of evidence" from the personality assessments and other measures, along with the fans' enthusiastic embrace of death metal, "suggest that the dramatic differences in emotional and aesthetic responses between fans and non-fans are genuine.

Chris Pervelis, a founding member and guitarist of the band Internal Bleeding (whose songs include *Gutted Human Sacrifice* and *The Pageantry of Savagery*), is confident that the positive emotions he experiences when he plays and listens to death metal are the real thing. "When I'm locked into it, it's like there's electricity flowing through me," says the 50-year-old, who runs his own graphic design business. "I feel really alive, like hyper-alive. And the people I know in death metal are smart, creative, and generally good-hearted souls."

In an essay published in August in *Physics of Life Reviews*, Thompson and his co-author Kirk Olsen considered the possible role of brain chemistry in the response to violence and aggression in music. The high , fast tempo and other discordant traits of death metal, they write, may elicit the release of neurochemicals such as epinephrine–which "may underpin feelings of positive energy and power reported by fans, and tension, fear, and anger reported by non-fans."

As for the central riddle of death metal–how explicitly violent music might trigger positive emotions in some people–Thompson cites a 2017 paper on the enjoyment of negative emotions in art reception, published in *Behavioral and Brain Sciences*. The paper, from the Max Planck Institute for Empirical Aesthetics, suggests a mental process that combines "psychological distancing" and "psychological embracing." In other words, a lack of real-world consequences–it's just a song!–may provide the *distance* necessary for fans to appreciate the music as an art form and *embrace* it.

A large body of research, by Anderson and others, has established a clear link between aggression and multiple types of media violence including video games, film, television, and music with violent images and themes. "But no one is saying that a normal, well-adjusted person–who has almost no other risk factors for violent behavior–is going to become a violent criminal offender simply because of their media habits," says Anderson, whose research includes a 2003 study of the effect of songs with violent lyrics. "That never happens with just one risk factor, and we know of dozens of common risk factors. Media violence happens to be one."

One finding from Thompson's research–that many death metal fans say they listen to the music as a catharsis, a way to release negative emotions and focus on something that they enjoy–is also familiar to Pervelis. "I call it the garbage can," he says of the music he's been involved with for decades, "because it's where I can dump all my bad, emotional baggage. I put it into writing riffs and letting it all out on stage, and it keeps me level and completely sane."

In his ongoing study of violent and aggressive music, which includes a June paper in the journal *Music Perception* about the intelligibility of death metal lyrics (forget about it, non-fans), Thompson has found that the limited appeal of the form may be one its key features for fans—one at least as old as rock itself. He cites a 2006 paper by the late Karen Bettez Halnon, who found that fans of heavy metal (as has certainly been the case with many other genres and sub-genres over the decades) view the music as an alternative to the "impersonal, conformist, superficial, and numbing realities of commercialism."

In that vein, one possible function of the gruesome lyrics that are the hallmark of death metal, says Thompson, may be to "sharpen the boundary" between fans and everybody else. Pervelis, who compares the violent imagery to the "over-the-top, schlock horror films of the '70s," says feeling like an outsider and an insider at the same time is at the core of the death metal experience. "This music is so extreme and so on the fringe of the mainstream that people who listen to it and people who play in death metal bands belong to an elite club. It's like we've got a little secret, and I think that's what binds it all. It's a badge of honor."

About the Author

David Noonan is a freelance writer specializing in science and medicine.

The Sound of Passion

By Patricia Moreau

Imagine a quiet night like any other. Suddenly, your infant's cries break the silence. Fully loaded with emotion, the sound triggers an urge to stand up and run to your infant's room. But, considering that your spouse is a musician and you are not, who will be the first to reach the crib?

According to Dana L. Strait and a team of researchers at Northwestern University in Illinois, the musician should win the race. Their latest study showed that years of musical training leave the brains of musicians better attuned to the emotional content, like anger, of vocal sounds. Ten years of cello, say, can make a person more emotionally intelligent, in some sense. So the alarm carried in a baby's cry make a deeper impression; your spouse wins the race.

The new work is part of an emerging portrait of the broader connections between music, emotion, and speech. These studies are finding that musicians are more accurate in detecting emotion–such as joy, sadness, and anger–in speech samples. The effect has been found even in children as young as 7 years old, with as little as one year of music training. It is a fascinating example of how experience in one domain (music) benefits another (emotion perception). However, it is not until very recently, with the publication of the new study by Strait and her colleagues, that the biological foundation of the effect has been demonstrated.

Strait's team decided to study the brain's very first responses to sound, in the brain stem. The brain stem is the most ancient part of the brain, and is the main entry door for all sensory stimuli. Once a sound reaches the nerves in your ears, it travels to the brain stem to be processed in an automatic, unconscious fashion. Both music and speech thus start their journey to the higher brain regions through the brain stem.

To record brain stem responses, the researchers placed electrodes on the heads of 30 people who were either musicians or nonmusicians. The electrodes measured the electric currents that send signals through the brain stem, while the participants listened to an infant's unhappy cry.

The surprising result was that the musicians' brain showed enhanced responses to the infant's cries. And the greater the number of years of practice and the earlier the person began training, the stronger the signal.

But how can musical training account for musicians' advantage in detecting vocal emotion? Strait and her colleagues suggest that as we engage in activities that involve high levels of cognitive processing, such as memory or attention in music, we also enhance our sensory system's responses. The higher brain areas in the cortex are connected to lower brain areas, such as the brain stem, and, through these connections, the two areas influence each other.

However, there is still the question of causality: Does musical training really affect the brain or could it be that musicians are simply born with a different brain–that they are naturally drawn to music by their cognitive strengths? Another study suggests that musical training really does drive changes in the brain. Daniel J. Bosnyak and a team of researchers at McMaster University in Hamilton, Ontario, demonstrated that the brain responses of a group of non-musicians could change as a result of their participation in a just two weeks of training to perceive pitches accurately.

With the emergence of brain imaging technologies, our understanding of the effects of music training on the brain has been advancing rapidly. For example, we now have clear evidence of morphological changes in the brain, such as enhanced volume in the cortical motor representation of the hands of string players or larger gray matter volume in parts of the musicians' auditory cortex dedicated to pitch processing. Numerous studies have also identified differences in patterns of brain activity between musicians and non-musicians. However, even with all this building evidence, we are still far from understanding exactly how music reshapes the structures and activity of the brain.

Surprisingly, even with all the remaining questions regarding musical training, the field of neuroscience of music has even more challenges to face. Although music processing has fascinated neuroscientists for more than a century, it is only in the last decade that it has become a subject of intense and systematic research. Aside from the effects of musical training, many more aspects of music, such as how we perceive it, how we enjoy it and how we make it, have been under the scope of researchers. There is general agreement that the brain is tuned for music, but untangling the complex circuitry behind the wondrous experience of it will require more research in this young and rich field.

About the Author

Patricia Moreau is a doctoral student in neuropsychology at the International laboratory for Brain, Music, and Sound (BRAMS) at the University of Montreal. Her research focuses on the biological foundation of congenital amusia, a developmental disorder defined by difficulties in producing and appreciating music.

Making Creepy Music Gives You Goose Bumps

By Amanda Baker

I have opinions about scary music. Years as part of a local haunted house has left me able to identify horror tracks from movies I've never seen. I not only know who Midnight Syndicate is – I have preferred albums. But figuring out what makes music scary takes more than just hours logged in a pitch-dark maze; it takes science.

It isn't hard to believe that music can affect your emotions; most people have their preferred songs from when they are feeling down or need to get amped before a big day. Movie soundtracks take it a step further and help audiences know where they are and how they should be feeling. Are they hopeful in Middle Earth or anxious in a galaxy far, far away? Or maybe, like in the recent *A Quiet Place*, silence itself can be the most powerful soundtrack.

But how does one kind of music tell audiences the big kiss is coming and another tell you that the killer is hiding behind that closed door? One group of researchers teamed up with a composer to create soundtracks with different acoustic qualities. Part of their inspiration came from animals in distress. Mammals in distress produce sounds that are non-linear and can have increases in pitch. Other animals, including humans, pay attention because such sounds are designed to stand out and send a message of distress.

The researchers were not going to just record animal screams–though some famous horror soundtracks apparently wove them into their scores. They created musical pieces with the critical acoustic qualities instead. They produced 10-second music selections, some of which had non-linear components at the halfway point. The added instrumentation changes or stimulated distortion marked a shift from the expected, linear quality leading up to that point. Participants listened to the clips and rated them for whether they were emotionally stimulating and if they felt happy or sad. The soundtracks with the distortion were more emotionally stimulating and generally received more negative ratings.

But sound only goes so far. Other researchers found differences in brain signals in the amygdala, hippocampus, and other areas when presenting pleasant music versus dissonant music. Importantly, the activation was greater when visual and music cues were presented together. Removing visual cues altogether can affect the experience as well, like the researchers who found increased reactions in people whose eyes were closed during the experience. But what about when the visual and auditory cues are in conflict? The researchers from the first study paired their 10-second clips with mundane videos and compared it to reactions to the music alone. When the discordant music cues were paired with a trivial moment–like someone turning the page of a book–the difference in arousal was suppressed. It's not just about the right sound, but the power of the right visual (or lack thereof) to go with it.

Cutting the soundtrack for our haunted house was a huge endeavor. You had to pick the right music, figure out how long certain things would take, decide if changes would happen at a certain time or had to be triggered, decide which moments would be cues for the cast, and overlay the sound effects. Maze music is not the same as ghost-in-the-room music, and neither of those are the same as person-breaking-in-through-the-window-during-a-storm music. The music was also loud, because it had to cover the sounds of moving set pieces and cast members working behind the walls. At critical moments, it also kept the people in the group from being able to hear each other, isolating them. But when we asked people at the end about the music, most said that they couldn't remember any. They sometimes remembered how loud it was when they entered the first room, but after that they noticed only sound effects–the breaking glass, thunder, a music box. But we can hardly consider all of the work creating the ominous and discordant sounds as wasted, they just blended so well as to fade to the background of the whole experience. As classic as certain horror soundtracks are, sometimes the best music is the kind that no one remembers.

The views expressed are those of the author(s) and are not necessarily those of Scientific American.

About the Author

Amanda Baker is a science communicator and outreach advocate. She has a geoscience PhD from Cornell University and has managed open-access, academic journals as well as the outreach journal Frontiers for Young Minds. *She is currently writing and editing science content for kids, from curriculum materials to magazines like* Smore. *She has served as a Science Olympiad national event supervisor and taught a first-year writing seminar on sustainable earth systems while at Cornell.*

In Teen Music Choices, Anxiety Rules

By Abigail Baird

In 2009, Miley Cyrus reportedly made an astonishing $25 million. Most of that money came from album sales, which were reported to be slightly over 4 million during that year. Four million...4 million?! Have you heard Miley Cyrus sing? Are there really 4 million kids out there willing to spend their hard-earned babysitting money on a Miley Cyrus album because they deeply love listening to her sing? Well, according to the findings of a study recently published in Neuroimage, selling 4 million albums does not translate to having 4 million people like your music. The study reports that there is good reason to believe that a lot of those purchases were made out of fear–a fear well known to adolescents all over America: terror of social rejection.

The fear of social rejection is so strong in adolescents because their relationships are essential for passing on the lessons that will enable them to join adult society. In order to do this properly and efficiently, teenagers come equipped with the ability to learn fast and furiously from their peers, especially those who wield more social power or who are older or more popular. Although this system developed because it helps the teen transition to adulthood, it has proven an excellent principle upon which to base economic decisions. The popular kids dictate teen culture, and if they endorse it (*Twilight*, anyone?) it will sell.

Gregory S. Berns, the chair of neuroeconomics at Emory University, and his colleagues set out to understand more about the neural and behavioral mechanics of social influence on decisions about purchasing music. The researchers' basic question was: When people change their behavior based on social influence, is it their actual preferences that change, or simply their behavior? In order to investigate this question they designed a clever behavioral study that was amenable to being performed while participants had their brains scanned.

The researchers chose to study adolescents between the ages of 12 and 17, a cohort thought to be highly susceptible to social influence, and known to buy at least one third of albums in the United States. Each participant heard a short clip of a song downloaded from the social networking site Myspace. Following the clip they were asked to make two ratings, one indicating how familiar they were with the clip (which was always the hook or chorus of the chosen song) and one indicating how much they liked the clip on a five-point scale. The clip was then played a second time, and they were again asked to rate how much they liked the song. However, in two thirds of these second trials the teens were shown a popularity rating that was estimated based on the number of times the song was downloaded.

When no information about the popularity of a song was displayed, teens changed their likability rating of the song 12 percent of the time. Not surprisingly, after being shown the popularity of a song, teens changed their ratings more frequently, on average 22 percent of the time. This difference was highly significant, and it is worth noting that among those who changed their likability ratings, 79 percent of the time teens changed their ratings in the direction of the popularity rating–they followed the crowd.

These behavioral findings validate a great deal of previous research on conformity, and demonstrate that it is alive and well in the average American adolescent. Although these results are compelling, they do not address whether or not teens were actually "following the crowd" or, upon further reflection and information from their peers, changed their intrinsic preference for a particular piece of music. To investigate this question, Berns and his colleagues looked to brain activity.

Their logic was simple. Using the first rating of the songs, it would be possible to find a network of brain regions that related to individuals' reports of liking the music. If, after they changed their minds in the second rating, this network appeared again, then it would suggest that the adolescents really did change how much they liked the music based on the influence of their peers.

If, on the other hand, a different network of regions revealed itself following a change in likability rating, this would be more in line with the notion that teens were simply complying with their peers.

Liking of songs, based on teens' initial ratings was strongly related to activity in the head of the caudate nucleus. Although the exact nature of caudate activity remains a source of debate, most agree that activity in this area is highly related to reward and valuation. So it appears to reflect pleasure, not familiarity. The researchers also observed activity in a number of regions that have been previously associated with the pleasurable aspects of listening to music.

When adolescents changed their ratings, according to their brain activity, it had nothing to do with increased liking of the music. Instead, a very different picture emerged. The network of regions associated with changing a rating included bilateral insula, the anterior cingulate cortex and the supplementary motor cortex and frontal poles–regions previously associated with anxiety and pain. These regions all showed increased activity when teens were shown a popularity rating that did not match their own, meaning that they had this neural response prior to changing their own rating. Interestingly, individuals who demonstrated the greatest sensitivity to popularity, as determined by survey measures taken at the beginning of the study, manifested the strongest insula activity during the act of conforming. Simply, the greater the insula activity, the higher the odds of conforming. The authors suggest that this pattern of activity can be explained by cognitive or emotional dissonance caused by the mismatch between one's ratings and the ratings of others.

So, the authors argue, conforming seems to be motivated not by the positive utility of behaving like your peers, but instead out of anxiety and pain at the prospect of being a "contrarian." Again, this points to the function of peer influence during adolescence. During adolescence, peers wield considerable coercive power–that is, friends are quick to dispense disapproval, teasing, and rejection when social norms are not followed. The pain of being rejected by one's peer group can be a matter of life or death, as recent cyber-bullying cases in the news demonstrate.

So what does this study mean practically? Well, there are very different implications for commerce and parents. In terms of marketing, if you want to sell a lot of albums, get the popular kids hooked, and their endorsement will cause enough fear among their overly attentive peers to make the music sell. The idea of being able to relate to another teen for only $12.95 is very appealing to adolescents, who are consumed with trying to maintain their status in their peer groups.

For parents the implications are a little different. Take heart from these findings. It is likely the case that your teenagers do not actually like the terrible music you hear during those brief moments when they take their ear buds out. In fact, the researchers found that adolescents who were most sensitive to the ratings of others engaged in much less active listening (which is particularly encouraging given the lyrics of some popular music). The bottom line for parents is that if your adolescents' need for the latest Hannah Montana album keeps them in step with their peer group, take it as a sign that they are aware of their culture—and this type of conformity is often predictive of a teen eventually becoming a well-adjusted adult.

About the Author

Abigail Baird is an assistant professor of psychology at Vassar College who studies brain development in adolescence.

Why Music Moves Us

By Karen Schrock

As a recreational vocalist, I have spent some of the most moving moments of my life engaged in song. As a college student, my eyes would often well up with tears during my twice-a-week choir rehearsals. I would feel relaxed and at peace yet excited and joyful, and I occasionally experienced a thrill so powerful that it sent shivers down my spine. I also felt connected with fellow musicians in a way I did not with friends who did not sing with me.

I have often wondered what it is about music that elicits such emotions. Philosophers and biologists have asked the question for centuries, noting that humans are universally drawn to music. It consoles us when we are sad, pumps us up in happier times, and bonds us to others, even though listening to an iPod or singing "Happy Birthday" does not seem necessary for survival or reproduction.

Some scientists conclude that music's influence may be a chance event, arising from its ability to hijack brain systems built for other purposes such as language, emotion, and movement. As Harvard University psychologist Steven Pinker famously put it in his 1997 book *How the Mind Works* (W. W. Norton), music is "auditory cheesecake," a confection crafted to tickle the areas of the mind that evolved for more important functions. But as a result of that serendipity, music seems to offer a novel system of communication rooted in emotions rather than in meaning. Recent data show, for example, that music reliably conveys certain sentiments: what we feel when we hear a piece of music is remarkably similar to what everybody else in the room is experiencing.

Emerging evidence also indicates that music brings out predictable responses across cultures and among people of widely varying musical or cognitive abilities. Even newborn infants and people who cannot discern pitch enjoy music's emotional effect. "Certainly music seems to be the most direct form of emotional communication," opines renowned neurologist Oliver Sacks of

Columbia University, author of the recent book *Musicophilia* (Knopf, 2007). "It really seems to be as important a part of human life and communication as language and gesture."

Such dialogue provides a way for people to connect emotionally and thus may reinforce the ties that underlie the formation of human societies, which have clear survival advantages. Musical rhythms may have even facilitated certain physical interactions such as marching or dancing together, further cementing our social ties. In addition, tunes may work to our benefit on an individual level, manipulating mood and even human physiology more effectively than words can—to excite, energize, calm, or promote physical fitness. All these benefits are causing people to reconsider whether music is truly as frivolous as it seems.

Mosaic in the Mind

Throughout recorded history, people have attempted to explain music's sway over the human spirit. Music has been labeled everything from a gift of the heavens to a tool of the devil, from an extension of mathematics to a side effect of language processing. Charles Darwin was famously stumped by music's ubiquitous presence around the world: man's predilection for music, he wrote in 1871 in *The Descent of Man*, "must be ranked among the most mysterious with which he is endowed."

Since the 1950s many psychologists have attempted to explain music's power by comparing music appreciation with speech. After all, an understanding of both music and speech requires, at its most primitive level, the ability to detect sounds. The brain's auditory cortex, an area dedicated to hearing, is now known to process basic musical elements such as pitch (a note's frequency) and volume; the neighboring secondary auditory areas digest more complex musical patterns such as harmony and rhythm. [For more on how the brain processes music, see "Music in Your Head," by Eckart O. Altenmller; *Scientific American Mind*, January 2004.]

In addition, language and music both contain a grammar that organizes smaller components such as words and musical chords, phrases made up of melody or prosody (the melodic line of speech), and tension and resolution. Indeed, music has been found to excite brain regions involved in understanding and producing language, including Broca's area and Wernicke's area, both located in the left hemisphere on the surface of the brain. (The majority of people process language mainly in the brain's left hemisphere but encode most aspects of music in the analogous regions on the right.) Thus, musical syntax–for instance, the order of chords in a phrase–could have arisen from the mechanisms that evolved to organize and understand grammar.

But tunes also recruit other brain systems, principally perhaps those governing emotions such as fear, joy, and sorrow. For example, damage to the amygdala, the brain's fear hub, impairs a person's ability to feel scared and, in some studies, sad in response to song. Many modern researchers thus conjecture that music evolved by piggybacking on a unique constellation of brain regions dedicated to language, feelings, and other functions. "I think there's a very good chance that music is simply a side effect of things that evolved for other reasons," says auditory scientist Josh McDermott, now at New York University.

Universal Language

Music's simultaneous activation of diverse brain circuits seems to produce some remarkable effects. Instead of facilitating a largely semantic dialogue, as language does, melody seems to mediate an emotional one. When a composer writes a lamentation or a toddler exuberantly bangs out a rhythm on a pot, that person is not only revealing his or her own emotional state but also causing listeners to share those feelings. Several pieces of research indicate that music reliably conveys the intended emotion in all people who hear it. In the late 1990s neuroscientist Isabelle Peretz and her colleagues at the University of Montreal found that Western listeners universally agree on whether a song using Western tonal elements is happy, sad, scary, or peaceful.

Music's emotional content may even be culturally transparent. This past April neuroscientist Tom Fritz of the Max Planck Institute for Human Cognitive and Brain Sciences in Leipzig, Germany, and his colleagues exposed members of the Mafa ethnic group in Cameroon who had never heard Western music to excerpts of classical piano music. The researchers found that the adults who listened to the excerpts consistently identified them as happy, sad, or scary just as Western listeners would. Thus, the ability of a song to elicit a particular emotion does not necessarily depend on cultural background.

The musical tongue may also transcend more fundamental communication barriers. In studies conducted over the past decade, cognitive psychologist Pam Heaton of Goldsmiths, University of London, and her research team played music for both autistic and nonautistic children, comparing those with similar language skills, and asked the kids to match the music to emotions. In the initial studies, the kids simply chose between happy and sad. In later studies, Heaton and her colleagues introduced a range of complex emotions, such as triumph, contentment, and anger, and found that the kids' ability to recognize these feelings in music did not depend on their diagnosis. Autistic and typical children with similar verbal skills performed equally well, indicating that music can reliably convey feelings even in people whose ability to pick up emotion-laden social cues, such as facial expressions or tone of voice, is severely compromised.

Recently, in a clever experiment, acoustics scientist Roberto Bresin and his co-workers at the Royal Institute of Technology in Stockholm garnered quantitative support for the idea that music is a universal language. Instead of asking volunteers to make subjective judgments about a piece of music, scientists asked them to manipulate the song—in particular, its tempo, volume, and phrasing—to maximize a given emotion. For a happy song, for instance, a participant was supposed to manipulate these variables by adjusting sliders so that the song sounded as cheerful as possible; then as sad as possible; then scary, peaceful, and neutral.

The researchers found that the participants—expert musicians and, in another study, seven-year-old children—all landed on the same tempo for each song to bring out its intended emotion, be it happiness, sadness, fear, or tranquility. These findings, which Bresin reported at the 2008 Neuromusic III conference in Montreal, bolster the idea that music contains information that elicits a specific emotional response in the brain regardless of personality, taste, or training. As such, music may constitute a unique form of communication.

Choral Bonding

Music's ability to convey feelings may underlie one of its most important benefits. In most cultures, music is almost always a communal event: everyone gets together to sing, dance, and play instruments. Even in Western societies, which uniquely differentiate musical performers from listeners, people enjoy music together in a wide variety of settings: dancing at a wedding or a nightclub, singing hymns in church, crooning with their kids, Christmas caroling and singing "Happy Birthday" at a party. The popularity of such rituals suggests that music confers social cohesiveness, perhaps by creating empathetic connections among members of a group.

But empathy may not be the only means by which music facilitates unity. Studies show that when people listen to music, the motor regions of the brain are also active—probably for the purpose of processing rhythm. These include premotor areas, which prepare a person for action, and the cerebellum, which coordinates physical movement. Some researchers have a hunch that part of music's power stems from its tendency to echo and synchronize our activities. "I can see how rhythm and physical action would have mutual resonance in the nervous system," speculates neuropsychologist Robert Zatorre of McGill University. "All sound is produced by movement. When you hear a sound, it's because something has moved."

Then it is a small step from walking, breathing, and hearing a heartbeat–natural rhythmic sounds that are not intrinsically musical–to purposely keeping time or matching another's gait. "Part of the reason music works is that when you hear a pattern, you can join in. You know how to organize your muscles to produce the sound you are hearing," Zatorre explains. In this way, the rhythm of a song could also serve as social glue by promoting a kind of physical bonding.

The idea that music may promote a type of nonverbal togetherness gains additional support from a 2008 study by neuroscientists Nikolaus Steinbeis of the Max Plank Institute for Human Cognitive and Brain Sciences and Stefan Koelsch of the University of Sussex in England. Steinbeis and Koelsch used functional magnetic resonance imaging to pinpoint a brain area that responded to chords but not to words, in a task in which volunteers listened to both. The responsive region turned out to be the superior temporal sulcus, a part of the brain's surface near the ears that responds to nonverbal social cues such as nonspeech vocal utterances, eye movements, and body movements. The activation of this region hints that music may indeed be helping to forge social ties.

Whatever its origin, such cohesiveness is extremely valuable to a communal animal such as ourselves; traits that enhance such unity tend to persist. "Music is usually a social activity," Koelsch explains. "While people make music, they communicate and cooperate with one another. In a way, they practice social activity and social functions. This social behavior is highly important for the human species."

Musical Medicine

Music also bestows advantages on us as individuals. Underlying our conscious impressions of a tune are physiological effects that can improve our mental and physical well-being. Studies show that upbeat, tense, or exciting music can physically excite the listener, triggering the body's fight-or-flight response: heart and breathing rates increase, a person may break out in a sweat, and adrenaline enters the bloodstream. This "pumping up" effect explains why so many people enjoy listening to rock or hip-hop while they work out–the music primes the physiological systems needed for high-energy movement. The psychological effect is important, too; music is a welcome distraction, making exercising more fun. Energizing melodies tend to boost mood in general, waking us up if we are feeling tired and creating a sense of excitement in any situation.

On the other hand, music can be calming, reducing the levels of the stress hormone cortisol in the blood, lowering heart and respiration rates, and alleviating pain, according to several studies. The classic example of this anxiety-reducing effect is a mother soothing her baby to sleep with a lullaby. In addition, clinical studies have shown music to be a powerful tool for relaxing patients about to undergo surgery, controlling their pain, and ameliorating behavioral issues in children and people with dementia.

In 2000 gerontology researcher and nurse Linda A. Gerdner of the University of Arkansas for Medical Sciences exposed 39 severely impaired Alzheimer's patients to music they liked twice a week for six weeks. The favored music, as determined by a questionnaire, reduced the patients' agitation levels during and after the listening period much more than did a similar schedule of classical "relaxation" music they heard at a separate time. Beloved music also has been found to reduce pain during surgery and child labor. The analgesic effect apparently outlasts the listening: exposure to music during labor or a medical procedure can lessen the soreness experienced afterward, even after the music has stopped.

And of course people self-medicate with music all the time. Broad surveys have found that nearly everybody reports listening to music by themselves for the purpose of enhancing or altering their emotional state.

Built for Song?

Given its undisputed allure, might music have some unique roots in the brain in addition to piggybacking on other systems? Researchers have described several cases of brain damage that impaired a person's capacity to feel emotions inspired by music but not by other stimuli. Lawrence Freedman, a friend of Sacks's, selectively lost his passion for classical music after a concussion from a bike accident. Freedman could still recognize the classical works he used to love, Sacks says, and he was still moved by visual art and other experiences, but music gave him no pleasure. Presumably the accident damaged a part of the brain dedicated specifically to enthusiasm for music, although no one knows exactly what part of the brain that is.

Other researchers argue that music has independent origins because the capacity to appreciate it appears to be hardwired at birth. Various studies show that infants pay rapt attention to song and even seem to prefer song to speech. In preliminary findings published in July 2008 in *Nature Precedings*, neuroscientists Maria Cristina Saccuman and Daniela Perani of Vita-Salute San Raffaele University in Italy and their colleagues showed that music activates regions in newborns' brains similar to those activated in more mature listeners. Saccuman and Perani used fMRI to see how the brains of one- to three-day-old newborns responded to classical music and found a pattern that mirrored music processing in adults: the infants' right hemisphere auditory system responded more strongly than the left. The researchers also altered the music by either making a section in the middle of the excerpt suddenly jump into another key or playing the entire musical segment in clashing keys. These more jarring passages preferentially activated the infants' left inferior frontal cortex, an area implicated in musical syntax processing in adults, and the limbic system, the seat of emotional response, just as happens in adults. "The brain seems to be born ready to process music," Saccuman concludes.

This innate readiness for music is thought to be tied to the phenomenon of motherese, the peculiar singsong way people instinctually talk to babies. The universal use of motherese has led some experts to speculate that it may be the original starting point for both music and language. Some experts, notably cognitive archaeologist Steven Mithen of the University of Reading in England, theorize that language and music both evolved from a musical protolanguage that our hominid ancestors used. Neandertals and other extinct hominids appear to have vocal chord structures that suggest they could sing, according to Mithen. Ancient humans certainly played instruments: researchers have uncovered bone flutes that are tens of thousands of years old.

The truth is that we may never know why music exists; evolutionary theories are very difficult to test. But even amid uncertainty about music's origins, we can still use songs to pump ourselves up or calm ourselves down, ease pain and anxiety, bond with others, or simply move people to tears. "Music is the most direct and mysterious way of conveying and evoking feeling," Sacks professes. "It is a way of connecting one consciousness to another. I think the nearest thing to telepathy is making music together."

Referenced

Music and the Brain. Norman M. Weinberger in *Scientific American*, Vol. 291, No. 5, pages 88–95; November 2004.

Sweet Anticipation: Music and the Psychology of Expectation. David Huron. Bradford Books, 2006.

Comparing the Processing of Music and Language Meaning Using EEG and fMRI Provides Evidence for Similar and Distinct Neural Representations. Nikolaus Steinbeis and Stefan Koelsch in *PLoS One*, Vol. 3, No. 5, e2226; May 21, 2008.

Music in the First Days of Life. Daniela Perani et al. in *Nature Precedings*, online preprint July 29, 2008.

Universal Recognition of Three Basic Emotions in Music. Thomas Fritz et al. in *Current Biology*, Vol. 19, No. 7, pages 573–576; March 19, 2009.

About the Author

Karen Schrock is an editor at Scientific American Mind.

GLOSSARY

amplitude The measure of the height of a sound wave, which is what affects how loud it is.

auditory Relating to hearing.

consonant When two or more tones combine to create a harmonious and pleasing musical sound.

dissonant When two or more tones combine in a non-harmonious way to create tension in music.

electroencephalogram (EEG) A test that measures brain activity by using small metal discs to measure electrical activity.

entrainment When an organism becomes synchronized to an external rhythm, such as music.

evocative Bringing to mind strong memories, associations, or feelings.

musicologist A scholar who studies music in relation to other academic disciplines, such as history, sociology, psychology, and the sciences.

neurological Relating to or affecting the nervous system, including the brain.

pitch How high or low a sound is based on the speed of vibrations that produce it.

progenitor An ancestor, something from which something else is descended.

salient Most important.

tonality The relationship between the arrangment of notes, keys, pitches, and chords in a musical work.

FURTHER INFORMATION

Affo, Marina. "Learning to Love Music," Neuroscience News, April 2, 2023. https://neurosciencenews.com/asd-music-therapy-22923/.

Dreher, Diane E. "How Music Can Help Us Heal," *Psychology Today*, February 21, 2023. https://www.psychologytoday.com/us/blog/your-personal-renaissance/202302/how-music-can-help-us-heal.

Fan, Shelly. "The Ancient Marriage between Music, Movement, and Mood,' *Scientific American*, November 18, 2013. https://blogs.scientificamerican.com/mind-guest-blog/the-ancient-marriage-between-music-movement-and-mood/?.

Hamilton, John. "Building a Better Brain Through Music, Dance, and Poetry," NPR, April 3, 2023. https://www.npr.org/sections/health-shots/2023/04/03/1167494088/your-brain-on-art-music-dance-poetry.

Iqbal, Abdullah. "Music on the Brain: Listening Can Influence Our Brain's Activity," Ars Technica, September 24, 2022. https://arstechnica.com/science/2022/09/can-we-manipulate-our-mental-capacity-with-music/.

Schiffman, Richard. "The Healing Power of Music," *The New York Times*, April 8, 2021. https://www.nytimes.com/2021/04/08/well/music-therapy-treatment-stress.html,

Solis-Moreira, Jocelyn. "Research Shows Promising Effects of Music on Brain Power," *Discover*, February 1, 2022. https://www.discovermagazine.com/mind/research-shows-promising-effects-of-music-on-brain-power.

Spitzer, Michael. "The Neuroscience of Loving Music," Big Think, January 29, 2023. https://bigthink.com/series/explain-it-like-im-smart/your-brain-on-music/.

CITATIONS

1.1 Music Changes the Way You Think by Daniel A. Yudkin, Yaacov Trope (June 24, 2014); 1.2 The Sound Track of Our Minds by Nikhil Swaminathan (August 3, 2007); 1.3 What Makes a Song? It's the Same Recipe in Every Culture by Jim Daley (November 21, 2019); 1.4 The Beat Goes Off: Scientists Pinpoint the Loss of Musical Perception by Erin Hare (October 31, 2016); 1.5 Music Synchronizes the Brains of Performers and Their Audience by Robert Martone (June 2, 2020); 1.6 Play It Again, Sam by Susana Martinez-Conde (September 28, 2018); 1.7 Exploring the Musical Brain by Kristin Leutwyler (January 22, 2001); 1.8 Music And The Brain by Norman M. Weinberger (September 1, 2006); 1.9 Inner Spark: Using Music to Study Creativity by Alicia Anstead (May 1, 2011); 2.1 Music Lessons Combat Poverty's Effect on the Brain by Simon Makin (May 1, 2014); 2.2 Hearing the Music, Honing the Mind by The Editors (November 1, 2010); 2.3 Music Helps Kids Read by Jenni Laidman (May 1, 2014); 2.4 Rhythm and Music Help Math Students by Sophie Bushwick (March 27, 2012); 2.5 Does Music Boost Your Cognitive Performance? by Cindi May (March 3, 2020); 2.6 Everyone Can Gain from Making Music by Julia Calderone (March 1, 2015); 2.7 Fact or Fiction?: Babies Exposed to Classical Music End Up Smarter by Nikhil Swaminathan (September 13, 2007); 2.8 Math, Music and Imagination by Marcus Miller (April 13, 2018); 2.9 You Don't Have to Start Young to Be a Great Musician by Cindi May (May 21, 2021); 2.10 Even A Few Years Of Music Training Benefits The Brain by Christie Wilcox (August 21, 2012); 2.11 Speaking in Tones: Music and Language Partner in the Brain by Diana Deutsch (July 1, 2010); 3.1 "Alive Inside" Shows How Music Can Break Through the Fog of Dementia by Annie Sneed (July 18, 2014); 3.2 Heart Beat: Music May Help Keep Your Cardiovascular System in Tune by Lynne Peeples (June 24, 2009); 3.3 Music May Orchestrate Better Brain Connectivity in Preterm Infants by Christopher Intagliata (May 28, 2019); 3.4 How Music Can Literally Heal the Heart by Elaine Chew, Psyche Loui, Grace Leslie, Caroline Palmer, Jonathan Berger, Edward W. Large, Nicolò F. Bernardi, Suzanne Hanser, Julian F. Thayer, Michael A. Casey, Pier D. Lambiase (September 18, 2021); 3.5 Music Can Heal the Brain by William Forde Thompson, Gottfried Schlaug (March 1, 2015); 4.1 Let's Get Physical: The Psychology of Effective Workout Music by Ferris Jabr (March 20, 2013); 4.2 Why Does Music Make Us Feel? by Mark Changizi (September 15, 2009); 4.3 It's the Bass That Makes Us Boogie by Karen Hopkin (December 9, 2022); 4.4 Is a Sad Song Sad for Everyone? by David Noonan (January 6, 2020); 4.5 Dissecting the Bloodthirsty Bliss of Death Metal by David Noonan (October 30, 2018); 4.6 The Sound of Passion by Patricia Moreau (June 16, 2009); 4.7 Making Creepy Music Gives You Goose Bumps by Amanda Baker (October 24, 2018); 4.8 In Teen Music Choices, Anxiety Rules by Abigail Baird (March 16, 2010); 4.9 Why Music Moves Us by Karen Schrock (July 1, 2009)

Each author biography was accurate at the time the article was originally published.

INDEX

A

amusia, 18–20
Armstrong, Louis, 90

B

Bach, Johann Sebastian, 93
Beethoven, Ludwig van, 21, 49, 71, 93, 97
brain, 12–14, 18–23, 25–30, 33–43, 45–48, 52, 55–56, 61–64, 66, 75–80, 84, 90–91, 95, 99, 103–112, 118–120, 137–139, 141, 143–145, 147, 149, 152–154

C

chords, 8–10, 14, 55, 80, 149
cognition, 24, 27, 32, 34, 61–63, 72, 95, 103, 109, 138, 145, 147
contour, 28, 35, 81, 83
creativity, 43–48, 61, 68
culture, 14–16, 27, 33, 69, 104, 116, 128, 130–131, 133, 147, 150–151

D

dance, 14–15, 21, 23, 90, 108–109, 116, 125–128, 148, 151
Darwin, Charles, 14, 17, 148
dementia, 25, 90–91, 103, 108–109, 153

E

emotion, 10, 19, 21, 24, 29, 31, 40–41, 48, 60, 69, 83–84, 90, 98, 100, 109–110, 112, 116, 118, 121–123, 129–138, 140, 145, 147–151, 153–154
empathy, 22, 63, 133, 151
evolution, 14, 27, 30–31, 33
exercise, 76, 115–120, 153

H

harmony, 8, 36, 68–69, 148

I

improvisation, 43–49
interval, 8, 41

K

key, 16, 28–30, 154

L

language, 14, 17–18, 27, 31, 34–35, 40, 54, 56, 61–62, 68–69, 76, 78–83, 85–87, 103–104, 107, 110, 123, 147–150, 154–155

M

math, 32, 55, 57, 61, 68–70, 76, 148

melody, 10, 14–15, 21–22, 28, 36, 38, 40–41, 68, 73, 79, 81–83, 99, 104–107, 111, 117, 119, 149

memory, 12–13, 19, 38, 40, 51, 54, 61, 63–64, 90–91, 105, 109, 112, 116, 119, 138

Mozart, Wolfgang A., 54, 61, 65–66, 71, 95

P

phrasing, 10, 30, 150

pitch, 10, 14, 16, 18, 26–29, 31, 36, 54, 62, 73, 75, 81–83, 85–87, 110–112, 123, 138, 148

practice, 39, 50, 54, 59, 62–64, 68, 71–74

prosody, 81, 84, 149

psychology, 8–9, 14, 25, 60, 62–63, 78, 116

A

Ravel, Maurice, 25–26, 34

reading, 52, 62, 76, 79, 84

rhythm, 10, 15–16, 18, 21–22, 26, 28, 30–31, 36, 56–57, 68–69, 73, 81, 93–94, 97, 99, 104, 106–108, 116–117, 123, 125, 148–149, 151–152

S

Schubert, Franz, 21, 98

T

tempo, 14, 28–29, 61, 81, 83, 93, 108, 116, 120, 123, 134–135, 150–151

timbre, 10, 16, 28, 36, 62

tone, 10, 14, 16, 32, 36–37, 85–87, 111–112, 126, 150

V

Verdi, Giuseppe, 93, 99